Darryl's
We hope our story
encourages you along
in your own paths!
Blessings,

Neil and Kate

Maria

Jack Megan

Rhoda

a.g.
Luke

Proverbs 16:9

The Invitation

An Adoptive Family's Memoir

Kate and Mark Skidmore

WestBow
PRESS
A DIVISION OF THOMAS NELSON

WestBow Press books may be ordered through booksellers or by contacting:

WestBow Press
A Division of Thomas Nelson
1663 Liberty Drive
Bloomington, IN 47403
www.westbowpress.com
1-(866) 928-1240

Because of the dynamic nature of the Internet, any Web addresses or links contained in this book may have changed since publication and may no longer be valid. The views expressed in this work are solely those of the author and do not necessarily reflect the views of the publisher, and the publisher hereby disclaims any responsibility for them.

Any people depicted in stock imagery provided by Thinkstock are models, and such images are being used for illustrative purposes only.
Certain stock imagery © Thinkstock.

Cover Photo and Authors Photo © 2008
Classic Photography by M. Chris Leese
www.mchrisleese.com

Scripture taken from the HOLY BIBLE, NEW INTERNATIONAL VERSION®. Copyright © 1973, 1978, 1984 Biblica. Used by permission of Zondervan. All rights reserved.

ISBN: 978-1-4497-0906-8 (sc)
ISBN: 978-1-4497-0907-5 (dj)
ISBN: 978-1-4497-0904-4 (e)

Library of Congress Control Number: 2010941417

Printed in the United States of America
WestBow Press rev. date: 1/6/2011

For our children
Jack, A.J., Rhoda, Maria, Megan, and Luke.
We are so thankful for the gift of you…each of
you and all of you!
You can be confident that you are a part of a
divinely designed family.

For children everywhere in need of a forever
family.

Preface

This is an account of our family's "invitation" to adopt two Ugandan orphans, Rhoda and Maria. A key purpose in writing this story is for our six children and our future grandchildren to have an account of how our family came to be. In addition, we have been asked many times about our story, but that requires more than a thirty-second explanation. Now when people express an interest in hearing the full account, we can share a copy of this book.

As we wrote this book, the original purposes expanded as we came to realize that our story represents a shift in the paradigm of how our society perceives adoption. It is our hope that by sharing our journey, other families will find their forever children—the ones that grow right in their heart. While adoption is not for every family, we agree with Mac Powell from Third Day who said, "Adoption is for more people than have acted so far to date."

Last, we believe that the hand of Providence reaches into all of our lives. In documenting our story, we hope to heighten sensitivity to the invitations presented in the lives of others so that they will be moved to join God in His work; to experience the abundance that comes from taking steps in faith. Some people see our family and remark how fortunate Rhoda and Maria are to have found a place in our family. Those who have been touched by love will understand that we are all the lucky ones. When taken in by love, it is a privilege to walk through life together, to share unconditional love, to love one another through our imperfections, to encourage each other through life and its challenges, and to participate in what we experience as our divinely designed family.

Acknowledgments

The Invitation is our story. However, we want to acknowledge that our story could not be told without the many amazing people who have gone before us, responding to the invitations in their own lives. Though this list of people is far from comprehensive, we feel compelled to acknowledge those who encouraged us along the way and prepared us to respond to our invitation.

Thanks to our parents who raised us to think about community and family with a much broader perspective. We extend our heartfelt appreciation to our mentors who introduced us to a personal relationship with God through Jesus Christ. A special thanks to my sister, Elizabeth Shepler, and her husband, Scott, who had already responded to their adoption invitation. We also acknowledge the support we received from our family and friends who walked with us as we worked our way through our experience.

Thanks to Mandy Sydo for her example and willingness to respond with an all out YES when she inherited the Welcome Home Orphanage from her close friend Jackie Hodgkins following Jackie's death after a short battle with cancer. We also express our appreciation for Momma Jackie Hodgkins who saw a great need and responded by establishing the Welcome Home Orphanage as a way to "To Love, Care, and Pray Babies Back to Health; or into Jesus Loving Arms." Thanks to David and Victoria Crowhurst who cared for a tiny baby they found under the tree near their Ugandan home. We are thankful for the name they gave to Rhoda, the love they shared, and needs they met to ensure that Rhoda had a loving start in life. We also extend our gratitude to the staff at Welcome Home, the loving care they share daily with the children entrusted to them has eternal significance.

We are humbled by the love extended by the Reidmiller family, who stepped into their adoption invitation with the willingness to take on a life of service in loving and caring for beautiful Yvonne, while already experiencing less than ideal personal circumstances. May God's grace cover each step they take along the way. We also thank Meadow Merrill, along with baby Ruth, for navigating the adoption path out of Uganda and Kenya to the United States just prior to our journey with Rhoda and Maria. We thank her for writing about Ruth's story which was published in her area newspaper. Meadow also wrote about Mandy Sydo and the Welcome Home Orphanage; this article was published in the Reader's Digest Make it Matter online magazine (Article #80381). Reading her stories gave us the vision to share ours too. We extend our sincere gratitude to Naomi who voluntarily took time off from work to help us navigate the immigration process in Kenya. Our return home certainly would have been delayed considerably without her assistance and friendship.

We acknowledge all the families worldwide that have been moved to touch the life of a child in need of love, a home, and a family; because of their examples we have taken our step too. Thanks to Herb Morreale from Topplers.org. His question, "What can I do to help you write that book?" helped make the idea of writing this story a reality.

*Names with an asterisk have been changed to protect privacy.

Contents

Preface   vii
Acknowledgments   ix

Chapter 1   1
   Introduction   1
   The Ground Rules   2
   Just Living Life   3
   "I'm pretty sure I don't have what it takes."   4
   Pings   5
   Foreshadow   6

Chapter 2   9
   Face Full of Sunshine   9
   The Seed Grows   11
   The Girls   13
   Rhoda   15
   Rhoda's Health History   17
   Maria   19

Chapter 3   21
   Making Preparations   21
   Timing Is Critical   23
   The Trip Plan   25
   Last Minute Curveball   26

Chapter 4   29
   Day of Departure   29
   Arrival in Uganda   30
   Meeting Our Lawyer   31
   Jinja   33
   Phone Calls Home—The Adventure   34

Chapter 5   35
   Welcome Home Orphanage   35
   Meeting the Girls   36
   Life at the Orphanage   38

The Mums 39

Joseph 42

Orphanage Conundrums—Very Raw and Very Real 43

Phone Calls Home—Like a Breath of Fresh Air 45

Chapter 6 47

Visa Photos 47

Encountering Life in Uganda 48

The Goodbye Party 52

Phone Calls Home—Many Smiles 55

Chapter 7 61

The High Court 61

The Judge 61

From the Bowels 65

The Court Order 67

The Orphan Investigation 69

Phone Calls Home—That Was Encouraging 71

Chapter 8 73

Our Weekend in Purgatory (I mean Entebbe) 73

Embracing the Moment 74

The Zoo 76

Sunday Church 76

Time and Chance 78

Anxious Hours of Waiting 80

Phone Calls Home—A Cool Drink of Water 83

Chapter 9 85

Part-Time Angels 85

The Physicals 87

The British Embassy and the Airside Transit Visa 89

Chapter 10 95

Traveling Home 95

Home! 97

Redefining Normal 99

Chapter 11   103
   The Children Today   103
   What about MSU?   107
   In Closing   108
   An Invitation   110
Afterword   111
References   115

Chapter 1

"Whoever welcomes one of these little children in
my name welcomes me; and whoever welcomes me
does not welcome me but the One who sent me."
-Mark 9:37 _{NIV}

~ the Scripture verse, printed by Samaritans Purse, that hung on our
refrigerator for a number of years prior to the start of this story.

Introduction

At some point in my distant past, I recall sitting in a church somewhere in the Milwaukee area listening to a man share his family's story about adopting a child. While I don't remember the particular details, what stuck with me was what the man said about how their family began the adoption process. He and his wife didn't wake up one morning and say, "Today I think I will adopt a child." Rather, just like a natural pregnancy has a conception, adoption has a conception too.

Conception begins in the mind. It begins by thinking generally about the idea of adopting a child. Naturally, many questions come to mind: Why adopt? Should we adopt? How does one go about adopting a child? How much does it cost? When is the right time? Whom should we adopt? Along the way, these questions begin to transform the heart. Once this adoption seed is planted, it begins to grow, and at some point one receives what I call a divine invitation to act. It is in responding to this invitation that the adoption idea begins to become a reality.

This story is an account of how our lives and the lives of our children were transformed by a divine invitation to adopt two Ugandan orphans. It is a story of the people we met, the friendships we made, and the challenges we encountered. This is a story of how God invited us to join Him in His work, and how He led us to greater faith and maturity as He met our needs along the way.

The Ground Rules

Mark and I became engaged in February of 1996 after a brief period of dating. During our engagement, we had many different conversations about important issues as we prepared to enter into marriage. As with most couples, one topic we discussed was children. We agreed that we were open to growing our family, but neither one of us felt that we absolutely had to have children. If we decided to pursue having kids, we were in agreement that we would consider both the old-fashioned, natural-born method and/or adoption. As Christians, we believe that we are all adopted into the family of God. It was this belief that made thinking about adoption an easy thing to consider early on in our relationship. This adoption concept is articulated in Romans chapter eight:

> "For as many as are led by the Spirit of God, these
> are Sons of God. For you did not receive the Spirit
> of bondage again to fear, but you received the Spirit
> of adoption by whom we cry out, Abba Father."
> -Romans 8:14-15 NKJV

In addition, Mark grew up in a family that was torn by alcoholism and divorce. During that tumultuous period, other families took him in and sort of "adopted" him. Being grateful to the families, teachers, coaches and friends for the extra love, help, and encouragement that he received throughout those difficult years, it was natural for Mark to find ways to pass it on.

One conviction I held about adoption was that if we ever adopted outside our own race, I would want to bring in two children of similar likeness, not just one. My thinking was that two adoptive siblings who share similar physical characteristics might feel more grounded and thus experience a stronger feeling of belonging within the adoptive family.

As for the total number of children we would each consider, there were some minor differences. I was willing to consider between two and four kids, but Mark could only imagine two or three kids.

These were the basic ground rules about children and adoption that we carried into our marriage; the very beginning of our adoption conception, so to speak.

Just Living Life

After our wedding on August 2, 1996, we went about building our lives the way our hopes, dreams, plans, and circumstances led. We began our marriage by spending our honeymoon year in Nagoya, Japan. Mark had put himself through college, ultimately earning a Ph.D. in economics from the University of Colorado. I tease him that he is the only person I know who *accidentally* ended up with a Ph.D. He had originally applied to the master's degree program, but was accepted to the Ph.D. program. He figured that he might as well see what he could do to meet the challenge. Mark has a way of taking on challenges and overcoming obstacles. Whether he was working to get his 5'7" frame high enough into the air to slam dunk a basketball, earning a starting position on his junior college basketball team, rejecting his college advisor's recommendation that he **NOT** major in economics, or learning tough lessons about publishing academic research, Mark makes the most of his assets and opportunities. When you first meet Mark you might miss his intensity because of his steady, unassuming and good-natured personality.

Just months before our paths crossed, he had applied to become a Fulbright Scholar to Japan. Mark's Fulbright opportunity, along with some divine inspiration, was a catalyst that moved our relationship in a period of just ten days from, "Would you like to go on a date?" to "I don't know about you, but the way I see it, we should get married. It's just a matter of sooner or later." Mark didn't want to go to Japan without me. All of this was a shock to our friends and family—it was so out of character for both of us. When Mark made the announcement to his best friends and men from his weekly Bible study, they exclaimed "We didn't even know you had a girlfriend!" Mark just smiled and said while rubbing his fingers together in the air, "You know when you know."

After a year in Japan, we returned home to DeKalb, Illinois, where Mark continued working at the university and I spent the year finishing a master's degree. During the summer of 1998, we each found new jobs, packed our bags, moved to Wisconsin, and built a house. We were beginning to feel settled in our marriage, lives, location, and employment. In addition, I was pushing thirty and Mark was nearly four years older…it was time to begin thinking about starting a family. Our first child came quickly. Jack Thomas Skidmore was born December 30, 1999, two days before Y2K. It also happened to be Mark's thirty-fifth birthday! We spent New Year's Eve 1999 in the hospital and returned home a couple of days later with our new baby in the new millennium…the beginnings of a new adventure.

Over the next four years we welcomed two more natural-born children into our family. Andrew James Skidmore was born April 5, 2002, and he was followed by Megan Mckenzie Skidmore on April 30, 2004. This baby thing, though hard on the body, brought joy to my soul.

We were three kids into growing our family. From my logical build-a-family brain, our family was beginning to feel complete. We even got "the dog" just after Megan turned one. The timing for families getting a dog generally follows two rules. A young married couple gets a dog to see if they are really ready for a baby, or more seasoned couples with a few kids get a dog when they're done having kids. Having a dog is like having a permanent toddler around anyway, so who needs more kids, right?

"I'm pretty sure I don't have what it takes."

Our lives were full and fun, and we seemed to be managing the care of our children well. Even so, three kids in four years was a pretty fast pace, and we thought it might be wise to slow down a little and catch our breath. After all, we had our "more than two but less than four kids." We even managed to sneak a girl into the predominately male Skidmore line.

I recall saying to Mark in one conversation, "You know, I just don't think I will ever have what it takes to actually adopt. I like the idea of adopting, but now that we have three children, I just don't see that idea ever turning into action."

It was as if, when those words left my mouth, God chuckled to himself and said, "Ahhh. Finally, they are ready. I don't want adoption to be their plan; I want it to be unmistakably **MY** plan."

Pings

If this had been the first divine appointment or "ping" experience in my life, I might have missed it and moved along. But this was not the first ping I had heard. I am a person of faith. My definition of faith is to experience life with an understanding and confidence that life is bigger than what I can see or touch. My faith acknowledges a hand that guides me. I cannot see or physically hold this hand, but it is instrumental in influencing the direction that my life has taken. Though I do not audibly hear any messages, I sometimes experience a pressing in or what I refer to as a "ping."

I have received several pings in my life, but in my earlier years I was rarely brave, confident, or wise enough to listen to and trust in them. Over time, as I have grown in my understanding of God and have strengthened my relationship with Christ, I have gotten better at trusting Him. Admittedly, I am still not very good at it, but I attempt to live "by faith and not by sight." I use the term ping, but others might describe it as a call from the Holy Spirit. Regardless of the language one uses to describe such experiences, my sense is that these promptings provide an opportunity for us to respond. Many Scripture verses confirm that the Holy Spirit guides each of us and plays an active role in our lives. As one example, the Apostle Paul and his partner Barnabus received a call from the Holy Spirit:

> "While they were worshiping and fasting, the
> Holy Spirit said, "Set apart for me Barnabus

and Saul (Paul) for the work which I have called
them….The two of them, sent on their way by
the Holy Spirit, went down to Seleucia and sailed
from there to Cyprus." –Acts 13:2,4 _{NIV}

One ping led me to graduate school; another brought me to a church where I met Mark; the biggest divine appointment up to this point in my life was how Mark and I met and shortly after became engaged. Though I wasn't prepared for where this adoption ping might lead us, I was committed to doing the leg work, confident that God was in charge of moving things into or out of our lives.

Foreshadow

As we wrote this story, it was fun to think back on our lives and the many experiences we'd had. Separately, each experience isn't overly significant, but taken together they reveal a pattern and a larger plan. Looking back, we saw all the lessons and how these experiences changed our hearts. A vision for our future was formed out of these experiences and helped to prepare us to take action when our adoption invitation was presented to us.

During the summers of 1992–1995, I worked at a camp called "The Challenge Program," where I led groups of kids on ten-day outdoor challenges. We would backpack, canoe, work on service projects, and participate on high and low ropes course elements with the goal of building teamwork, trust, and self confidence. Over the course of my four summers leading groups, I learned that group dynamics with kids were most effective, interesting, and entertaining when there were at least six but not more than ten kids, preferably with an even number in the group.

Another experience that prepared us early on was the writing of our wedding vows. While we had written them independently, we both captured the desire for our life together to have a positive impact on the world. In my vows to Mark I wrote, "It is my hope that with God's hand being a part of our life, that we will live a life that is so full of love and sharing that it will naturally spill over into the lives of the people we meet."

Mark's vows to me included, "I believe God has drawn us together for His pleasure and purpose. I know that together we will become more than we could apart, and together we will serve God more fully." In order for us to seriously consider adoption, both of us would have to be in full agreement.

One other foreshadowing experience was our decision to sponsor a child through World Vision. When Jack was four and A.J. was two, we decided to sponsor a child. Jack and I spent an afternoon searching the pictures on the World Vision website for a boy his age who we could sponsor. We wanted someone to whom we could write and send pictures and maybe, someday, have the opportunity to meet. We decided on Jonal, a three-year-old boy from the Dominican Republic. Jonal's picture, which was posted on the refrigerator, was a constant reminder, and Jack wondered when we would get to meet him and bring him over for a visit to our house. Though Jonal had a family, I think the idea of bringing a child (or children) into our home slowly began to seep into our thoughts and hearts, including Jack and A.J.

One of my favorite recollections is of an innocent conversation I had with Jack when he was about four years old. We were sitting at the kitchen table, and he said, "Mom, I want to have five brothers and sisters." I replied with a smile, "If you want five brothers and sisters, then you are going to need to find a different family." Even back then, when I spoke those words, there was a strange prick in my heart.

Chapter 2

Face Full of Sunshine

My sister Elizabeth served as the messenger for our divine invitation. Elizabeth and her husband Scott have two adopted African-American children. Since they were an adoptive family living in a small town, they had become part of an informal adoption network in their community. This connection resulted in Elizabeth placing a picture of a certain little girl on her bulletin board.

On July 11, 2005, we traveled to Elizabeth's home in Mineral Point, Wisconsin, to celebrate her son Joshua's sixth birthday. During our visit, I happened to look at her bulletin board and noticed two 8x10 pictures of three small Ugandan orphan girls. When I asked who they were, she replied, "This one is Yvonne. She is a girl who was recently adopted by a family we know."

The second picture was of two children playing in a toy car. The first child had a face full of sunshine, and right behind her was a second, quieter-looking child. My sister pointed to the first little girl in the car photo and said, "This is Rhoda. She has a brace on her leg, and they are hoping to find an adoptive home for her too." Elizabeth explained that in Uganda, Rhoda would not receive the medical care she needed and would likely live a shunned life because of her leg.

As the birthday party and activities continued, I gave little thought to the pictures or conversation, other than feeling sorry that a lack of access to medical care would leave this child with a limited future. To my surprise, later that day, I experienced a ping that seemed to whisper, "What about you?" I didn't pay any attention to it at first, but as the day wore on, in my mind and heart, I kept hearing that whisper: "What about you?" After the third or fourth ping, I thought to myself, *I'm fine. I'm good. I have three children ages five, three, and one. I'm good!* Another two or three pings later, I hesitantly decided to mention the whisper to Mark.

When I told Mark what I was feeling and sensing, his response was relaxed: "Why don't we e-mail the director of the orphanage and just ask a few questions?" This caused a surge of adrenaline to rush through my body. I had been married to Mark almost nine years, and things seemed to happen when we just asked a few questions. I knew how this worked.

The next day, Mark e-mailed Welcome Home Ministries—Africa to inquire about Rhoda. A reply came back saying that Rhoda was already in the process of being adopted by a different family.

Though curious about Rhoda, I quietly breathed a sigh of relief. I had done my part. I'd heard the ping, followed it up with questions, and found the answer was no. End of story, right?

Wrong.

About one month later, Mark and I were in the process of selling our 1992 Toyota Previa van and getting a newer Previa. While we were scouting out a newer van, I suggested, "Maybe we should consider selling our five-passenger car and just have two vans."

Mark blurted out, "That's it!"

"What's it?" I replied.

"I don't know why, but I don't think this thing with Rhoda is done."

"What makes you think that?"

"I don't have any idea, but I think we should sell the car and buy a second van because this thing with Rhoda isn't done."

At that point, I thought to myself, *I'm the one with stronger intuition. I haven't heard this message.*

The next day, Mark e-mailed Welcome Home again. "I just wanted to see how Rhoda's adoption is coming along. I am not sure why, but I wanted to check with you about her."

A short time later, we received an e-mail message from the director, Mandy Sydo: "Then we should talk."

What did that mean? My mind was reeling with both excitement and anxiety. Did that mean the other family was not going to adopt Rhoda? Was Mark right, and the possibility of adopting Rhoda wasn't over?

Later, Mandy called Mark and told him that the other family was having trouble deciding about Rhoda, so she was still in need of a home and family. Mandy's experiences with adoption had led her to believe that a family was either ready to adopt or not. Doubts and uncertainty were just too difficult to manage for everyone involved. As the character Yoda from *Star Wars* would say, "Do or do not; there is no try."

Mandy said she would call the next day to talk further. While Mark had been handling all the correspondence with Mandy thus far, he was away when she called again. With eager anticipation and butterflies in my stomach, I answered the phone and began to talk with Mandy. I had chills running up and down my spine as she described this little girl named Rhoda. I remember looking around the room, wondering whether I was in the presence of angels, as the conversation seemed very natural. I was very calm. At that moment, discussing Rhoda with Mandy was the same as talking about Jack, A.J., or Megan. I wasn't filled with the anxiety, doubt, or fear that I had expected, given that we were talking about the possibility of adopting a young girl with medical needs from the other side of the world.

The Seed Grows

Mandy lives in California when she is not in Uganda. But it happened that she was making a visit to Mineral Point, Wisconsin, to celebrate the final adoption of Yvonne, the other little girl whose picture had been on my sister's bulletin board. Two days after our phone conversation with Mandy, we were able to meet face to face to discuss the possibility of adopting Rhoda.

I wanted Mandy to meet all of us, including Jack, A.J., and Megan. It was important for her to understand what we were already managing. We also needed her to be candid about Rhoda and her health needs and to help us realistically assess our circumstances to see if Rhoda, with her challenges, would be appropriately served in our family. We felt that we had plenty of love to share, but we didn't want to take on more than we could handle.

In addition, we were considering the possibility of adopting a second child, so that Rhoda wouldn't be moving around the world alone. A.J. was three at the time, and I couldn't imagine sending him to Africa by himself. With these thoughts in mind, we asked if Rhoda had a healthy "friend" that we could also adopt. Mandy thought it was a very good idea for Rhoda to have a friend join her, but that piece would take some work because the current board policy for Welcome Home prohibited out-of-country adoptions for healthy children. She was hopeful, though, because she was still transitioning into her role as the new orphanage director, and there were some expected changes that might be ensuing.

After leaving our face-to-face meeting with Mandy, the best way I can describe our reaction was that we kept thinking about what to do next. We wanted to figure out how to get more involved. It was like experiencing a slow gravitational pull toward adopting Rhoda and her friend.

On August 16, 2005, I could see that my attachment with Rhoda was really beginning to take hold in my heart. Though she was not even with us yet, we decided to have a birthday party for Rhoda. She was turning three years old, so we baked a birthday cake, blew up balloons, and celebrated. We sang "Happy Birthday" and took pictures of Jack, A.J., and Megan holding her birthday cake. Even though Rhoda was still on another continent, we felt compelled to celebrate our soon-to-be daughter's birthday, as she was really becoming a part of the family. Today, that is one of her favorite stories to hear when we celebrate her birthday each year.

In early September 2005, we were beginning our home study, which is the first step in preparation for adoption. During some of the initial meetings, they asked us questions to determine whether we were a suitable family to adopt two children. As we answered these questions, there were times when anxious feelings stirred in my heart about the impact of adopting two older girls from Africa. I knew how important those years from birth to age three were from a developmental perspective, and I didn't want to negatively affect our already existing family. When I thought about adopting the girls from a purely logical perspective, there were times when I felt overwhelmed. Thankfully, I was free to bring my concerns to God because it was unwise to move forward with doubt in my heart. As I pondered these things, God met me with a kind whisper. He seemed to say, "Kate, you do not have to do this. This is simply an invitation. You frequently express your desire to be where I am working. There is a need here, and you are invited to join me." After receiving that calm reassurance, my doubt melted away, and we proceeded without delay.

Four months later, we had completed our home study and obtained approval to adopt both Rhoda and Maria (the friend sitting behind Rhoda in the picture of the toy car). We were doing our best to finalize the many details required before traveling to Uganda to meet the girls and bring them home. We now had two seven-passenger vans, which is exactly what a family with five children needs. Jack and A.J. were very excited about the idea of adding two more children to the family. Every day, the boys asked when we were going to pick them up. Megan was still too young to fully understand what was happening, but we knew she was going to make a great baby sister.

The Girls

With the adoption seed taking root in our hearts, we longed to know more about these two young girls. Neither Rhoda nor Maria had any known relatives. Rhoda had lived her entire life in the orphanage, and Maria had been at Welcome Home all but four months of her life. In Uganda, a country for which UNICEF estimates that fifteen percent of kids under the age of fifteen are without parental care, there are no government programs designed to serve the orphan population (UNICEF 2009). Had we not adopted them, the girls would likely have ended up in Watoto, an orphan mission of the Pentecostal Church of Canada, which has its home base church in Kampala.

Watoto is a large village-type orphanage for older children (six and older). The village consists of many small cinderblock houses that have three bedrooms, a large dining room, a kitchen, a shower, and a toilet. Each home typically houses eight orphans, one house mum, and her own children if she has any. The Watoto village, though not an adoptive home with a loving mom and dad, is the best of the extension orphanages available. They work very hard to give the residence a homelike feel. The children are given an upbringing with the hope found in the love of Christ, along with access to primary and secondary education right in the village. Proudly, the Watoto education is considered a notch above the public education available in Uganda. The Watoto village also offers some additional vocational opportunities. For example, those with vocal talent may be eligible to participate in the Watoto Children's Choir, which offers opportunities to travel to England, Europe, Australia, Canada, and the United States. Watoto prepares orphans to transition back into their communities once they come of age, and it is hoped that the future of Uganda will be influenced by the leadership of the Watoto-raised residents as they set about living their adult lives.

In the United States, access to education is often taken for granted. But in Uganda, education is generally a privilege provided only to some; without external financial assistance from mission-minded supporters, orphans are normally not granted such opportunities. We are thankful that the Pentecostal Church in Canada has brought this opportunity to the Welcome Home Orphanage "graduates." In Rhoda's case, though, while she might have received basic health care had she been placed in the village, she would likely have gone without the surgery and the physical, occupational, and speech therapy that she needed. This lack of medical attention for her leg would have hampered her function and independence and would have likely resulted in her being shunned once she was on her own.

Rhoda

According to Rhoda's birth certificate, she was born on August 16, 2002. We don't know the exact length of time between her birth and when she was found. The best guess from Victoria Crowhurst, the woman who discovered Rhoda bundled in blankets beneath what we refer to as the "Rhoda tree," is that she was just a few hours old. David and Victoria Crowhurst are a longstanding British missionary couple whose compound is located a short distance from the road that leads to the town dump. Rhoda had been placed at the entrance to the site. We have heard slightly different stories about where and how she was deposited under the Rhoda tree. Her medical records indicate that she was found in the dump itself, but Victoria Crowhurst reported that she found this beautiful baby girl dressed in a long flowered dress that was too big for her, wrapped in a bundle of blankets, and set underneath a tree just outside the entrance. Victoria felt that whoever put this baby in that location was trying to set her in a place where she would be discovered by someone passing through to deposit refuse. Even after a thorough investigation by the police in the Mukono district, beginning the very day she was found, there was no information as to who put her there or why. We don't know whether her birth mother is dead or alive. Abandonment of a child carries a stiff penalty: imprisonment. In addition, childbirth is one of the leading causes of death for Ugandan women. For these reasons, it seems likely that her birth mother is no longer living.

The baby was examined immediately and was found to be in good health. Victoria Rhoda Crowhurst took the liberty of bringing this baby girl into her home to feed her, hold her, love her, and give her a name. Victoria chose her own middle name, Rhoda, for the girl. The Crowhursts were not sure what they would do with the baby in the long run, but they decided they would keep her for a time and make sure she had what she needed. After a month of caring for Rhoda, they decided that the American run orphanage, Welcome Home in Jinja, would be a suitable home for Rhoda. Even after Rhoda went to Welcome Home, they visited her regularly and were committed to insuring that she was doing well and had everything she needed. We are thankful to both the Crowhursts and Welcome

Home for keeping Rhoda in their love and care until we could bring her home...to her forever family.

Rhoda was three when we began planning to bring her into our family, and we were curious to learn more about her personality. Mandy had told us that she was beautiful and charming, but that she also had a tendency to scream when she didn't get her way. She was a favorite to most of the staff because she was so full of sunshine and had a joyful song in her heart...most of the time. Yvonne's adoptive family, the Reidmillers, had met Rhoda when they were in Uganda to pick up Yvonne. They said that Rhoda was awesome. One of the teenage Reidmiller girls said that if they could have, they would have brought Rhoda home too.

At some point during our four months of adoption preparations, Mandy mailed us a short video clip of Rhoda. It was true that she was radiant and spunky, but the video also captured her screaming side. Since I had worked extensively with very challenging at-risk youth in an earlier career, her screaming didn't really concern me. Rhoda's personality was known, concrete, defined. I felt like she was a dynamic wysiwyg (what-you-see-is-what-you-get) kind of kid.

Rhoda's Health History

We knew some of the details of Rhoda's health history prior to traveling to Uganda, but it wasn't until after we returned home that we were able to obtain her complete health history from the orphanage. Reading through her records helped us put many of the pieces together and was invaluable to us as we began identifying what type of medical interventions would be necessary in the future.

We learned that at about seven months of age, Rhoda contracted a serious viral or bacterial infection that resulted in meningitis. Meningitis is an inflammation of the membranes that cover the brain and the spinal cord. If a person manages to survive this life-threatening infection, there is still another risk: In its defense, the body dispatches white blood cells to fight off the infection. In some cases, the white blood cells become "sticky" and clog the brain's third ventricle, which is what happened with Rhoda. The blockage prevented her cerebrospinal fluid (CSF) from flowing normally around the brain and into the basal cisterns. This resulted in an accumulation of fluid in the brain, a condition called hydrocephalus.

Fortunately, one of the caretakers who knew Rhoda well had noticed a slight increase in the size of Rhoda's forehead. This caretaker was a woman from the United States who had been away for a month. That month away enabled her to notice the subtle swelling of Rhoda's head and the beginning tell-tale sign of hydrocephalus, "the sunset eyes" caused by an expanding forehead.

They immediately brought Rhoda to the CURE International Children's Hospital of Uganda in Mbale. On March 6, 2003, she was diagnosed with Post Infectious Obstructive Hydrocephalus. On July 9, she had surgery to open up the third ventricle. During this surgery, called Endoscopic Third Ventriculostomy or ETV, the surgeon creates a hole in the floor of the third ventricle so that the CSF can drain into the basal cisterns, bypassing the blockage. In the United States, this type of hydrocephalus is typically treated by installing a shunt, which allows the excess fluid to flow through a catheter that is inserted into a ventricle in the brain and then drain into another body cavity and dissipate. Not only is this procedure very costly, but the unsanitary conditions in Uganda would only result in more infections. ETV surgery, on the other hand, is not often used in the United States because of its associated risks, but it proved to be a very effective procedure for Rhoda. Her head circumference returned to her original percentile trajectory within six months of the surgery, and follow-up CT scans have consistently indicated that her ventricles are stable with fluids draining normally. Since one is never technically cured from hydrocephalus, Rhoda will require long-term monitoring to ensure that the ventricles in her brain remain stable and the CSF is flowing properly.

Since Rhoda's original illness, there have been additional complications that didn't surface initially. Though we knew she had some trouble with her left leg, she was later diagnosed with Hemi Plegia Cerebal Palsy (CP). This means that there was some type of damage to a nerve center in her brain that affected her legs. The CP is significantly worse in her left leg than her right leg, though both are affected. About four months after we arrived home, we also discovered that she is completely deaf in her left ear, which was likely caused by the meningitis.

Rhoda's treatment for hydrocephalus was the beginning of an outreach ministry by Welcome Home. Welcome Home identifies village children with hydrocephalus and pays the transportation for the children and their mums to make the trip to the hospital for surgery and to attend the follow-up appointments. There are many children with this condition, and people come from near and far to the Welcome Home gate for assistance. Welcome Home then brings these children to CURE to see Dr. Benjamin Warf. Dr. Warf, the physician who treated Rhoda and thousands of other children, is world-renowned for his expertise in working with victims of Post Infectious Obstructive Hydrocephalus. CURE truly works miracles, saving the lives of hundreds of children every year.

Maria

Once we confirmed that Maria was to be the friend who would also join our family, we wanted to learn more about her. In the original car picture, she seemed so quiet. In another picture taken of the two girls, Maria was not smiling. I searched the Welcome Home website to see whether I could find any additional pictures of her. Occasionally, I would see her in a sea of faces, but it was not enough to get a fix on or clue about her personality. Mandy described Maria as quiet but capable. She also said she didn't really smile very much. I was hoping to learn a great deal more about this pretty, quiet, and seemingly somber girl before we traveled to meet her.

Maria had been born prematurely on February 18, 2003 at a small clinic in the Kibuye district, weighing just 3 lbs. 6 oz. There is no record of what happened to the woman who birthed her, but Maria was transferred to a larger nearby hospital where she spent two weeks gaining weight and stabilizing. When she was just two weeks old, Maria was taken to Welcome Home. Even though she had been born prematurely, she was a very robust baby and did not have any notable health issues.

In May of 2005 when she was fifteen months old, Maria went to a live with a Ugandan woman in a nearby village. In 2003, this woman had fostered another girl, but it was later discovered that the child had cerebral palsy and was therefore returned to Welcome Home. The foster mother then selected Maria, but when the social worker went out on a home visit to see how Maria was doing, Maria was not there. The mother wasn't there either. Maria and the woman's other children were found at a neighbor's house. This neighbor willingly took care of the children when the foster mom left for long periods of time. The social worker's report made it clear that the woman's instability and mental health issues prevented her from properly caring for Maria. Though much of the time she loved and cared for the children in her home, there were periods during which she was not attending to her duties. Initially, the Ugandan equivalent of Child Protective Services planned to return Maria to the woman, but the Welcome Home Director advocated on Maria's behalf, insisting that she remain at the orphanage as this was no longer a suitable foster care environment. In September 2005, after being away from the orphanage for four months, Maria was again living at Welcome Home. I felt badly that she had been through so much in her young life, but I was very glad that she would soon be coming home with us.

Though I tried to learn more about Maria's personality, I was not able to find out anything more than what Mandy had initially told me: She was quiet and capable, but she does not smile very much. I was so curious to meet her. When we finally met, I found that she was quiet, seemed capable, but did not smile very much. Sometimes still waters run deep; I would have to wait and see what surfaced in time.

Chapter 3

Making Preparations

Rhoda and Maria, though on the other side of the world, had found their way into our hearts and the hearts of our natural born children. We had completed all the necessary paperwork to satisfy both the United States and Ugandan governments. Our home study requirements and fees had been handled. All the upfront legwork had been completed in less than four months, a relatively short period of time by typical adoption process standards. We were thankful that we had completed our pre-travel requirements efficiently, and we were beginning to feel confident that everything was in place to travel.

While we were away, my mom would be caring for our three natural born children. If she needed any extra help, my sister lived just two hours away, plus we gave her a list of people who lived nearby that she could call. If for some reason my Mom needed to return home to Michigan during our absence, we arranged for Linda Brown, my friend and colleague from Blackhawk Technical College, to care for the children.

Linda Brown had been a part of my life for eight years. She had watched our family grow from zero to three, and now five, kids. She had seen me bring my kids into work every day and drop them off at the on-site daycare facility. She knew each of my children well and waved to them most mornings when they traveled through the corridors in the Bye-Bye buggy, a push cart filled with children from the Children's Learning Center. Fortunately, she was also familiar with my new routine of dropping Jack off at school on my way to work. Though I hoped she wouldn't actually be needed while we were away, it made me feel much better knowing that I had someone on call.

One priority we had before traveling to Uganda was to know exactly how to establish consistent, convenient, and hopefully affordable communication to the United States so that we could stay connected with Mom, Jack, A.J., and Megan. We wanted to know everything that was happening in their lives back home. It was very difficult for both of us, but especially me, to leave the other three kids home while we were gone for three long weeks. We kept trying to think of a way that our whole family could travel together on this special mission. There were several factors to consider: A limited budget, safety, diseases including Malaria, and the significant number of immunizations required to travel. With the age of the children and the potential size of our group (eight including Rhoda and Maria), we decided that it just wasn't feasible.

After accepting that Mark and I would travel alone while my supportive mother managed affairs at home, we needed to figure out how to best stay in touch. I asked Mandy Sydo how she managed to stay in contact with the folks back home when she was in Uganda. She recommended obtaining an international calling card through Penny Talk, an affordable option for making international calls. The drawback to holding an international calling card was tracking down public telephones. We might have some luck finding a public phone in Great Britain and maybe even in Nairobi, but not in Jinja where we would spend most of our time.

Cell phones were widely available in the United States and Great Britain, and even in Africa. With a bit of research, I was able to find a used Nokia cell phone with the network capability I needed along with three different SIM cards and power sources for each of the three countries we would be visiting. With the cell phone coupled with the Penny Talk card, we were confident that we would be able to call home.

Taking into account the time change (Uganda was eight hours ahead of the Central Time Zone), we planned to call at our bedtime in order to talk with mom and the children in the morning before they departed for school. We knew that morning would be a crazy time for my mom, so we would keep the before-school calls down to a couple of times per week. We could always call on the weekends if we wanted to talk to everyone longer.

In an attempt to make every step of mom's life back at home manageable, I assembled a comprehensive "Guide Book" to walk her through each step of every day. It included maps, phone lists, medical release forms, and instructions for calling my cell phone in Uganda from our home phone. There were also daily schedules with reminders about packing lunches and practicing instruments. We tried to make sure every base was covered, both for mom at home and for us while we were out of the country.

Timing Is Critical

Oftentimes in life, timing plays a critical role in how things turn out. Our story is no different. Over and over again, the timing of events had to be just so in order for all the pieces of our plan to come together.

In the preparation stage, we managed to carve out a narrow window of opportunity for us to spend a month in Uganda. We had to arrange for the care of our six year old (Jack), almost four year old (A.J.), and almost two year old (Megan). Up to that point, we had rarely been away from our children for any length of time. Mark had been away for a couple days to attend an occasional conference, and I had only been away for twenty-four hours or so for an anniversary getaway. Leaving our small brood for more than three weeks was a significant stress point for both of us. We planned meticulously so that we could return at the earliest possible date.

In addition to arranging for the care of our children, we needed to choose a time that would not interfere with significant work responsibilities. As a professor, Mark had to consider his teaching schedule. Fortunately, he was able to arrange a delayed start date for an Internet-based class he was going to teach. This opened a window of time for us to travel early in 2006, and we scheduled our trip for January 4 through January 25.

As our departure drew closer, we ordered and picked up $12,000 in U.S. currency, all crisp, new $100 bills. They don't take credit cards in Uganda, so we had to bring along enough cash to cover the adoption expenses. The stack was thick, and it was unwise to carry such a large sum in a purse, wallet, or suitcase, especially to a developing country. Mom and I sewed pockets on the inside of two t-shirts so that we could carry the money unobtrusively. We had arranged for my mom to arrive early so that we could take her through a week's worth of "training" so that she was ready to take the helm while we were away.

With the flight scheduled and all the plans in place, we were set to leave in just two days. There was only one major problem: Before traveling, the USCIS (United States Citizenship and Immigration Service) had to provide formal approval of the I-600A form to both the adoptive parents and the U.S. Embassy in Nairobi, Kenya, which handles the immigration process for all of East Africa. While we had received our copy of the approval by the middle of December, the U.S. Embassy in Nairobi had not. Leaving for Uganda without the needed approval might only result in wasted time and a lot of heartache. The advice from everyone we talked to was the same: Do not travel unless you have a verbal confirmation from the U.S. Embassy in Nairobi that they have received the I-600A form from the USCIS. We were warned that even though there was typically a two-week delay between the adoptive family receiving a copy and the other copy being received by the U.S. Embassy in Nairobi, it could take up to 90 days.

I called every day to see if the approval had arrived. In order to reach the embassy during business hours, I would call between midnight and 2:00 a.m. December 29, 2005…no, the approval had not arrived. January 2, 2006…no. January 3, 2006…still no. We were scheduled to leave our Whitewater, Wisconsin, home at 7:30 a.m. on January 4, 2006. If the confirmation didn't arrive, we would have to cancel the trip and wait five more months before our next travel window was available. Five more months! That seemed like an eternity considering the young ages of the children. We had prayed over the course of several months, asking for our path to be cleared and for all of the pieces to be processed smoothly. What would happen?

At just past midnight on the morning of our travel day, I prepared to make the call one more time. The household slept, and I sat in the loft office dialing the number using the international calling card, entering the forty or so digits to complete the call. Finally, the phone rang. A consulate representative answered, and I gave him our case number. With my head aching from the stress, my heart pounding, and my stomach in knots, I waited as he retrieved our file. I explained that we had received our copy of the approval over three weeks ago and were scheduled to fly out that very day. After what seemed like an eternity, he stated in a very matter-of-fact tone that the approval had arrived. Yes! What a relief. Our prayers had been answered, and we were on our way.

After the phone call, I was able to catch a few hours of sleep, resting peacefully knowing that we could actually travel when we woke up. We finished packing in the morning, and Mark pulled out the package of $100 bills hidden in the closet. As we tucked the stacks of $100 bills into the hidden pockets in our shirts, Mark said, "Can you believe we are doing this?"

The Trip Plan

One benefit I had gained from years of taking groups on wilderness trips was that I recognized the value of being prepared for the unexpected. I liked to consider possible scenarios and develop contingency plans. As we prepared to leave, I felt that everything was in pretty good order, including a number of contingencies. This is what we thought would happen:

January 4	-Take a shuttle from Whitewater, WI, to Chicago O'Hare Airport
January 5	-Travel to England and then Uganda (eight-hour time change)
January 6	-Arrive in Entebbe, Uganda, early in the morning

	-Meet Joseph* at the Airport -Drive to Kampala to meet with our lawyer -Go to the High Court for the adoption hearing in the afternoon
January 7-15	-Spend time with the girls to give them time to bond with us. Let them decide when they are ready to switch from staying at the orphanage to staying with us.
January 16	-Travel to Kenya
January 17	-Complete the Immigration Physicals
January 18-22	-Stay with the Rains family in Thika, Kenya. Go on a one-day safari on the weekend.
January 23	-Return to Nairobi to pick up the results from the Immigration physicals -DEPART FOR HOME at 9 p.m.!!
Jan 24, 2010	-Arrive in Chicago at noon

We built in buffers of time and money for each stage of the trip, so we were comfortable with our schedule even if we did experience a few delays or problems. I love a great plan...and then there is reality.

Last Minute Curveball

The day before we were to leave for Uganda, Mark received a letter from Michigan State University, inviting him to apply for a newly endowed chair position in the College of Agriculture and Natural Resources. As we discussed the letter, we had no idea how this opportunity might affect our lives. The possibility was exciting, and it would mean more income, but the timing seemed ironic. How was it that this letter just happened to arrive the day before we left for Uganda? With an application deadline the Monday after we were scheduled to return? As we prepared to leave, we suddenly had new questions to consider. Should we be open to the possibility of moving, given all that was happening? How would our lives change when we became a family of seven? How would Rhoda and Maria and the rest of the family manage the adoption transition? The letter inviting Mark to apply for the job added another layer of stress to an already stressful trip.

Chapter 4

Day of Departure

We left home on the morning of Wednesday, January 4. We drove to Janesville where we dropped Jack off at school with an extra hug and kiss, then made our way over to the VanGalder bus station. My mom dropped us off and we said our tearful goodbyes to three-year-old A.J. and one-year-old Megan. We would greatly miss the little "boogers," as my ObGyn called them. We rode the shuttle from Janesville to O'Hare Airport in Chicago, and from there we flew to London. We tried to catch a few hours of shuteye during our flight and again on a brief layover in Heathrow, Great Britain, before catching our flight to Entebbe, Uganda.

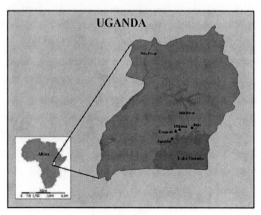

Uganda

Arrival in Uganda

Though we left the United States on Wednesday, with the time changes, it was early Friday morning when we arrived in Uganda. Our plane touched down as the sun was coming up, and the tropical air was still cool. We had been told that a man named Joseph* would meet us at the airport and take us to meet our Ugandan lawyer. Sure enough, Joseph had arrived and was ready to help.

Joseph was a tall, lean, dark man with a kind face. He worked for the orphanage and supervised most of the day-to-day activities. It is worth noting that Joseph was an expert driver. I had never thought to ask if the driver who would be carting us around Uganda was safe and capable. As it turned out, the roads were littered with potholes. Traffic was very congested, and in Kampala, only one of the traffic lights we encountered actually worked. In short, driving was a free-for-all, and thankfully, Joseph was very, very good.

We arrived in Kampala, the capital city, after a relatively short ride from Entebbe. Kampala, and more generally Uganda, is a little difficult to describe. As Mandy once told us, the people are still recovering from the suffering caused by the former dictator, Idi Amin. The people had been badly brutalized; the culture still seemed short on confidence and assertiveness, and yet there were pockets of transition with many successes. One such success was the transformation in communications that cell phone technology was bringing to Uganda. This transformation was a blessing for us as it enabled us to communicate with family back home and was a critical asset for helping us complete our business in Uganda.

Despite the progress, Kampala was chaotic and potentially dangerous. By nature of our skin color, we were marked as a likely source of money. Even though we were cautious, we were still a target. No one knew we were carrying $12,000 in cash, but we knew it, and that made us feel exposed. We tried to act as if nothing was unusual, avoided unnecessary exposure, and dressed in a way that gave the impression we didn't have any money. I did not wear any jewelry—no wedding band or earrings.

While we tried to stay together and cover ourselves, at one point Mark and Joseph needed to go into a building, and I was left alone on the city street with about $6,000 in cash. I stood with my backpack pressed against a brick wall, watching a tattered blanket full of disheveled looking adults and young children that appeared to be well versed in begging. I remember thinking to myself, *people have killed for much less than what I have on my body.* Though my fear was real, I couldn't help but feel compassion for the hungry bellies that likely haunted each of them on a daily basis. I could understand how real scarcity, especially of food, might lead people to steal in order to gain for themselves a morsel. Thankfully, I was left alone.

Meeting Our Lawyer

Joseph took us to meet our lawyer, David Lutalo*. His office was located in an older office building, up two flights of dirty stairs. The hallway was dark, and the heavy wooden door was marked "Lutalo" with one of those cheap plastic name plates. I was taken aback by the unremarkable setting. As we followed Joseph into the small, crowded office, the pungent smell of hot bodies and stale cigarette smoke hit me like a ton of bricks. I took small breaths through my mouth in order to avoid feeling nauseous.

The secretary barely looked up to acknowledge us when we entered. Her tiny desk, situated so that it mostly blocked the entrance to David's personal office, was crammed with an older computer and a large bulky monitor. The desk was the kind you might see thrown out in the dumpster of a college rental at the end of a hard four years of college. It was so small that the secretary had to hold her papers on her lap. Our entrance into the room brought stares and narrowed looks of inquiry from the people waiting: *What were these muzungus (white foreigners) doing here?*

After giving our names and a description of our business to the secretary, Mark and I left the office to go to the dark, dank bathroom so that we could pull out $8,600 from the hiding places in our clothes. We needed $5,000 to cover the legal fees and $3,600 for an advertisement fee, which included preparing and running a classified advertisement in the national newspaper as one last attempt to find any relatives who might make a claim on the children. We both felt ambivalent about handing over the cash. On the one hand, it was a relief to unload some money. On the other, we didn't exactly feel confident that all the pending legal matters would be resolved. So far, David hadn't yet completed the most critical parts of the work we had entrusted to him, and we knew we would need to rely on him heavily in the days ahead. All we could do was trust that Mandy Sydo and Joseph were right about David's ability to get the job done.

We returned to the suffocating waiting room and were called back to David's office immediately. Many of the people in the office were half asleep in their chairs, apparently having waited to see David for a very long time. We could almost feel the glares as we passed in front of them and squeezed past the secretary's desk into David's much nicer office.

David was a fairly tall and handsome man who dressed sharply. He exuded a strong ego, bordering on arrogance, befitting a high-powered lawyer. Walking into his office was like shifting realities. The room was nicely appointed with rich red carpeting and dark wood wainscoting that went almost halfway up the wall. In the center of the room was an impressive wooden conference table that matched the wainscoting. A ceiling fan hummed as it circulated the air around the room. It was just enough for the temperature in the room to feel comfortable.

David appeared distracted as he greeted us and shook our hands. We were invited to have a seat, and we sank into comfortable, plush chairs and waited for David to finish whatever it was he was doing when we arrived. After a short time, David shifted his attention away from his paperwork toward us.

The ensuing conversation wasn't exactly what we had expected. Our original plan was to go to the Ugandan High Court right away to complete the initial procedures necessary for adopting Rhoda and Maria. As we met with him that morning, David informed us that things had been delayed, and we would have to wait. We didn't exactly know why we had to wait, but we hoped that we would still be able to go to court early the next week. This was the first of many unexpected delays.

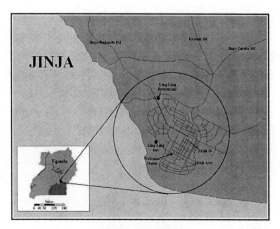

Jinja, Uganda

Jinja

After completing our initial business with the lawyer on the day of our arrival, we made our way from Kampala to Jinja. The city of Jinja is located about fifty miles northeast of Kampala, but it took about two hours to get there. Street-side markets selling anything from furniture to handmade drums to raw meat filled the roadsides, until we worked our way through to the true countryside where tea plantations and other crops dominated the landscape. As we drove into and through Jinja, Mark and I absorbed everything we saw.

Jinja is Uganda's second largest commercial center, with a population of more than 100,000. It is a relatively quiet and dusty city at the northern edge of Lake Victoria, the source of the Nile River. Jinja was established as a city in 1906, being transformed from a small fishing village to a center of commerce. At one time, there were significant East Asian and European populations in the Jinja area. With the foreigners and their investments, Jinja enjoyed relative prosperity. Then in 1972, Dictator Idi Amin expelled all immigrants from India. His bloody rule also led to the exodus of most Europeans, though they were not formally expelled. Under Amin's rule, so many bodies were dumped into Lake Victoria that the hydroelectric dam was often blocked by decaying human remains.

The once thriving city with its detailed Indian architecture fell into disrepair. Today, most of the shops are poorly maintained. The once beautiful colonial-style homes and plantations are now deteriorating, although many are still inhabited. Currently, the average annual household income in Jinja is equivalent to $100 U.S.

From our perspective, Jinja appeared to be a quiet city in disrepair. Despite evidence of some commercial activity, it was clear that poverty was present and the needs high. In response, there were a number of orphanages, one of which was Welcome Home.

Phone Calls Home—The Adventure

I called home today, excited to share about the adventure of traveling 8,000 miles around the world. I tried to describe the many sights, sounds, smells, and impressions of getting from Janesville, Wisconsin, all the way to Entebbe, Uganda. The kids seemed to enjoy hearing about how we road on a bus to the airport and flew in an airplane over the ocean. Jack found it fascinating that there were double-decker buses that drove on the "wrong" side of the road in London. At five years old, he is the only one of the children who seemed to fully comprehend what I was telling him. The others are really too young to "get" what I was saying.

I talked to my mom too. I told her all of the most interesting stories so that she could retell them to A.J. and baby Megan in a way that was meaningful to them. When I had three-year-old A.J. on the phone alone, he was happy to hear my voice repeating how much I missed him and that I loved him like crazy. I told him to point to the calendar on the refrigerator and count down the days until we would be home. Megan was very quiet when I was talking with her. Thankfully, when my mom first put the phone up to Megan's ear she said, "Momma!" Ahhhh. Her sweet voice was music to my ears.

Chapter 5

Welcome Home Orphanage

The Welcome Home Orphanage is a miracle. In Jinja and the rest of Uganda, poverty, disease, and violence have resulted in countless orphans. In addition, abortion is prohibited by law in Uganda. In much of world where abortion is legal, many social problems are "silenced" by the loss of millions of children every year. The critical objective for any society that chooses to protect life is to rise to the challenge of meeting the needs of a great many children. In the words of Horton in the movie *Horton Hears a Who* (2008), "A person is a person no matter how small."

The Ugandans work hard to meet the needs with very limited resources. Nevertheless, there is much suffering. Many children are abandoned, some in garbage dumps and pit latrines. All too often, children are neglected to the point of death. For example, one child we met during our stay had been rescued by an orphanage, but not before his toes had been badly eaten away by little worms called jiggers that enter the body as microbes, mature, and then eat their way out through the toes.

The mission statement of Welcome Home reads, "To love, care, and pray babies back to health; or into Jesus' loving arms." The orphanage provides a clean and safe environment for about sixty children. Importantly, the ratio of children to caretakers, or mums, is about three to one. This means that each child has a chance to be held and cared for, to receive love and affection.

Meeting the Girls

When we reached Welcome Home, all of the three- to five-year-old children, about thirty in total, were across the street from the gated orphanage with their mums playing on the red dirt soccer field that was covered with withered grass. I had rehearsed the moment of our first meeting many times, but I couldn't decide: Should I bring the camera or leave it in the car? Should we catch our first meeting on video or be live in the moment with no distractions? I finally decided that it was best to focus on the moment, free of all distractions, so we left the cameras in the car.

Joseph stopped the vehicle with my door at the curb. The mass of children recognized Joseph's car and all started yelling out, "Uncle Joseph. Uncle Joseph." I opened my door and stepped out onto the brick red dirt and began searching the faces for Rhoda and Maria. It didn't take me long to find Rhoda, face aglow and running with twisted steps toward me. She recognized me! I managed to walk a few paces and then kneeled to sweep her up into my arms and give her a great big hug. We were both delighted. Down on one knee hugging Rhoda, I scanned the faces right and left to find Maria.

"Where is she? Where is Maria?" I asked.

One of the mums pointed to my left. I turned my head to see Maria standing shyly waiting for me to get my arms around her too.

We had sent pictures of our family ahead of our arrival so the staff could explain to the girls who we were and why we were there. In an instant I could sense that they knew we were there for them. I had no idea where Mark was at that moment. I guess he was behind me watching and trying to move in close enough to get his arms around the girls too. The mums tried to shoo away all the other children, so that we could have a moment to hug and squeeze each other. As the crowd of children cleared out, Mark got close enough for the girls to see him. But when they saw him approach, they both let out blood curdling screams.

Joseph explained, "They are not used to seeing a white man, and they are afraid of you."

Surprised by their reaction and disappointed that he couldn't get in on the hugs, Mark backed away as I scooped both girls up into my arms. I carried them across the street to where the car was parked so that Mark could get the camera and take a few pictures.

At that point, we had been awake for twenty-seven hours, traveled over 8,000 miles, rode in a car for another three hours, and perspired in the sultry heat. I was straining to hold my two thirty-pound girls in my arms, but we managed to snap a couple of photos. Needless to say, I looked tattered and tired in those pictures. While I would have enjoyed having those first few minutes on video, I still replay our initial meeting over and over again in my mind. Rhoda and Maria love to hear the story, and it remains a favorite of theirs to share with others.

At first, both Rhoda and Maria looked wide-eyed at Mark and did not allow him to touch them. Any time he came too close, they would lean tightly into me. The other children in the orphanage, however, took to Mark quickly. We would go with the children across the street to play in the soccer field; Mark would sit down and soon be completely surrounded by a pack of little ones. They all just wanted attention and love. Imagine all the children, some with runny noses and dirty little fingers from all of the active play in the dirt, climbing and pawing on Mark. They were fascinated with opening and closing the zippers on his backpack. He didn't mind; he was enjoying the children, trying to give what he could.

With Mark's easy going personality, it only took a short time for the girls to get used to him. Rhoda was the first to warm up to Mark. Eventually, she flashed him a big smile and allowed him to pick her up. The real breakthrough came, though, when he put her up on his shoulders and went off on a jog down the soccer field. She loved it and was all smiles and giggles. When Maria saw that Rhoda was having so much fun, she wanted part of the action too. Cautiously, she approached Mark and allowed him to lift her onto his shoulders, and off they went. The connection between Mark and the girls had been made. All was well.

Life at the Orphanage

The first meal we observed at the orphanage was an interesting experience. While all the children had a good meal, how the meal got from their bowls into their bellies was a mixed bag. Some children made use of the utensils, while others scooped with their hands. Maria, even at the age of three (or not quite three), was very fastidious. She used her spoon as best she could and did not like the other children touching her bowl or cup. Rhoda, on the other hand, liked to scoop with her hand, shoving food into her mouth. Perhaps this was due to possible sensory delays that resulted from the illness she had experienced as a baby. In addition, both Rhoda and Maria had issues related to intestinal parasites, which consumed some portion of the calories and nutrients from the food they ate. The orphanage did a fine job of caring for the children, but given the environment, parasites were inevitable. If children carried parasites, they felt hungry more often. Perhaps Rhoda ate as quickly as possible in the hope that she might consume enough food to actually feel full. Just imagine, a little girl scooping up porridge in handfuls, vigorously shoving it into her mouth. She shoveled so quickly that she would sometimes gag on the mouthful of food. Mark and I looked at each other with wide eyes and raised eyebrows.

As we spent time getting to know Rhoda and Maria, we couldn't help but also develop connections with the other children in the orphanage. Some of the smiles that made their way into my heart belonged to Jamison, David, Rachel, Michelle, Amos, the triplets, Raymond, and Johnny. I could see that saying goodbye to the other children was going to be harder than I expected, especially Johnny. I even went so far as to ask if he was available for adoption. For us, there was something very special about him. The connection was in his smile, in his eyes; he had definitely worked his way into our hearts. Johnny's birth mother was alive, but she was very poor and was not able to care for him. As a result, Johnny ended up at Welcome Home. In principle I believe children should remain with their natural born families if at all possible. In this case, Johnny's mother was not able bring him home. We asked Mandy to let us know if his mother ever decided to relinquish her parental rights as we would strongly consider adopting him as well. Welcome Home offers to fund trips for her to come see him twice a year, but these visits rarely work out. To this day, we still ask about Johnny. He currently resides in a foster care home along with twenty-two other children. Mandy says that when she goes to visit him, it takes a long time for his shining spirit to emerge.

Back at Welcome Home, the children have a small pleasant yard in which to play. Donations from the developed world keep the entire facility in operation. In addition, there are specific donations targeted toward pieces of playground equipment, toys, art materials, and books that the mums use with the children during their morning school time. The children sleep in small bunk beds, about ten to each bedroom. You can imagine the difficulties in getting all sixty children to sleep at night! One tool the mums use is music from *Cedarmont Praise and Worship*. While this is a pretty energetic type of music and not something you would normally think of as calming bedtime music, somehow it works. The music drowns out the crying of other children, etc. It is common for the children's bums to be sticking up out of their beds, bouncing in rhythm to the music as they drift off to sleep.

The Mums

The mums at the orphanage all dress in simple smock uniforms. When not caring for the children, they live together in town at an apartment compound. Most of the mums share a small two-person bunk bedroom, about half the size of a typical college dorm room, and also have access to a common sitting room, bathroom, and kitchen facilities. In addition to their housing, they receive small salaries. Relative to other employment opportunities available to women, the arrangement is very good. For various reasons, none of the mums we met were married, although several had children of their own. In some ways, Welcome Home serves as an oasis for women who have been mistreated or somehow lost their grounding in society. Here are some snippets of what we learned about a few of the caretakers.

Mama Rachel* was a beautiful young woman, radiant and attractive even with the large scar that followed her hairline across her forehead. We were told that the scar was the result of a terrible car accident that she somehow survived. Rachel was the primary daytime caretaker for Rhoda and had a special relationship with her. Rachel loved Rhoda and cared for her during her illness. Rhoda still remembers and speaks fondly of Mama Rachel. Just recently, she wanted to write Mama Rachel a letter to tell her that she was doing fine and that she hoped to see her again someday. Mama Rachel, though very kind and pleasant, seemed melancholy. We learned that Rachel carried a very deep sorrow: When she was a young girl, she watched as her family was massacred in Rwanda. In a different conversation, we learned that she had a young child of her own, about Rhoda's age. Apparently, her husband had decided that he wanted to be with another woman and therefore abandoned Rachel. Given that the Ugandan culture and laws strongly favor men, Mama Rachel's own child had been taken from her. Moreover, the child had been given to the other woman, and Rachel was not granted permission to see her own child. I think Rhoda helped fill some of the hole in her heart. To this day, Mama Rachel enjoys reading Rhoda's progress reports. We send reports and pictures of the girls with Mandy when she visits twice a year. On Mandy's last visit, Rachel said she barely recognized Rhoda as she was growing up so fast. It is our hope that Rhoda and Rachel will maintain their special relationship throughout their lifetimes.

Mama Sue* was Maria's primary daytime mum. Among the caretakers, she was especially delightful. She was young and happy and seemed to operate without the presence of a heavy burden. Sue would pick Maria up, hug her and kiss her behind her ear and say, "I love Maria, but she is a strange girl. Her emotions are always so confused. She cries when she is happy and is happy when you think she might be sad. She wakes up at bedtime and tends to sleep late into the morning."

Mama Diane*, strong and simple, was another mum who had spent a lot of time with Rhoda and Maria in her role as lead teacher. She was also a very kind woman who had experienced extreme hardship. Her former husband was a cruel and jealous man. In an effort to destroy her natural beauty and make her less attractive to other men, he had poured acid on her chest. Amazingly, this was a fairly common practice in that part of Africa. Though she recovered from this extreme abuse, a large painful looking scar remains.

Mama Grace* was a little older than most of the other mums and appeared to be more stern. She was tall and thin, and her eyes reflected wisdom and determination. In addition to her responsibilities with the children, she was head of security and was charged with the duty of frisking every female employee at the beginning and end of every shift. This responsibility set her apart from the other staff. We could see that some of the younger staff both respected her and feared her. If Grace found an employee stealing from the orphanage, they would be terminated immediately. She had a strong presence, which helped keep order in the orphanage. Despite her more serious demeanor, Grace was very kind and was committed to caring properly for the children. By her standards, it was unacceptable for children to remain in dirty diapers for long, to have their clothes on backwards or inside out, or to go "su su" in the grassy play area. She tried to keep the children looking respectable, and she expected the same effort from the other mums, some of whom could be lazy. She was very capable. Mama Grace also had a child who was doing very well in high school, and she was making every effort to support her son and help him go to college. His future was uncertain, though, because resources were so limited. At one point, Mama Grace said to us, "Please don't forget us." We don't forget, but we wish we could do more.

Mama Barbara* was in charge of the daily schedule and spent a fair amount of time with both Rhoda and Maria. Mama Barbara was cautious toward us. She never fully warmed up to the idea of us taking the girls back to the United States, and there was a tension between us that never subsided. Barbara and a number of the other mums tended to keep their distance. This was a difficult thing for us to fully understand. Our instincts told us that mistrust served as a barrier. I could only imagine how I might feel if I were in their shoes. They loved the kids and cared for them, and we were swooping in and taking two orphans. Why were we taking these particular children to the United States? Why not some other child? What kind of people were we? From their point of view, it must have seemed arbitrary.

Another influence of note was Dede Elizabeth*. She and her husband, Pastor Richard*, were employed by Welcome Home. Pastor Richard taught the staff three times per week, and Dede Elizabeth trained all of the workers for the Welcome Home outreach ministry to the surrounding villages. In addition, she provided "Sunday School" to the children six mornings a week plus a worship time on Saturday. Most weekday mornings, she would teach the children about the love of Jesus and lead them in singing songs. As they sang, the children would also dance, shake the tambourines, and beat the drum. She would read Bible stories to the children as they leaned in to listen, thirsty for the message of love and hope. They would even watch an occasional video that Mandy brought over from the United States about a Bible character or Bible story. During one class while we were there, Dede Elizabeth taught them about Saul's conversion, how he became Paul, and how his life was changed by Christ's transforming love. When we picked up Rhoda and Maria, their hearts were filled with a special joy, a joy beyond their circumstances.

One of my favorite memories from Jinja is pushing the girls in the strollers down the red dirt road in the warm afternoon sun toward the inn where we stayed, with girls singing with their sweet voices, "The Joy of the Lord is my strength. The Joy of the Lord is my strength. The Joy of the Lord is my strength. The Joy of the Lord is my strength."

Joseph

Joseph serves as Mandy's Ugandan counterpart. He manages the affairs of the orphanage between Mandy's regular visits to Uganda, three to four times a year. As a manager, Joseph is level-headed and very capable. He maintains a calm demeanor even when faced with intense moments and crises. He manages most of the logistics at the orphanage, including food and baby formula orders, pick-up and delivery, communications, and the necessary paperwork for the government requirements and adoptions.

Joseph had started working with the orphanage in a position of limited responsibility, but he had increasingly earned the trust of Mandy Sydo and was promoted. Like many Ugandans, Joseph grew up in extreme poverty. Although he did learn to read and write, family challenges and limited means prevented him from completing his education. Nevertheless, Joseph was very sharp. He told us that he had hoped to follow the footsteps of his cousin, who had become a physician, but it was not to be. Nevertheless, his management position at the orphanage was a good one. It provided a reasonable salary, by Ugandan standards, which enabled him to care for his own family of four children, and Joseph was faithful in doing his part to care for the children at Welcome Home.

If Joseph had been born in the United States, I am certain that he would have obtained a college degree. He certainly had the raw abilities to become whatever he wanted. He might even have become a physician. But he was not born in the United States; he happened to be born in Uganda. Too often, those of us who grow up in the developed world attribute our successes to our personal efforts, as if we were responsible for it all. While I firmly believe in taking responsibility for our choices in life, it only takes a single visit to a developing country to see that the playing field is not level. The advantages and opportunities provided to so many of us here in the United States are overwhelmingly apparent when juxtaposed against the environment in which Joseph found himself. It seems wise to acknowledge and be thankful for the opportunities that come through no merit of our own, and not to take them for granted.

Orphanage Conundrums—Very Raw and Very Real

This was my first visit to an orphanage. Though I had seen images of orphanages in third world countries, experiencing one was very different. Pictures insulate you from sensory connections that are fully engaged when you are standing there in person. After entering the orphanage grounds through the heavy, black steel door at the guarded gate, Mark and I made our way into the children's yard through the small white picket fence at the front of the home. The pleasant but heavily-worn play area was stirring with activity. Teeters were tottering, children were swinging, and young voices were chattering with happy sounds. There in the front yard were the Mums and thirty to forty children between the ages of two and five. The other twenty or so toddlers and babies and their Mums were in the other play area in the backyard.

It was a sunny day in the middle of the dry season, so the children ruled the entire yard. As we walked through the area, we passed a line of ten to fifteen small plastic squat potties lining the sidewalk. These were for the older kids to use as needed and for the younger children to sit on as part of their group potty training sessions. Some of the children were thrilled to be able to take care of business sitting on their own little throne. Others, however, would sneak off into the large plants that surrounded the perimeter of the home and find relief *au natural.* Though the mums would quickly call them back to the potty chairs, often it was too late. Since I am a smell-sensitive person, the stench overwelmed me in a way that a picture never could. This was just one reality of a third-world orphanage. Here are a few other examples of the daily realities of orphanage management.

Dirt. Sixty kids get really dirty playing in brick red dirt every day. While it's hard to bathe sixty kids three times a day, Welcome Home is blessed to have enough water to provide small cold water bucket baths for the children. They get a bath when they wake up, after lunch, and again before bedtime.

Laundry. It is extremely hard to hand wash clothes and dirty bedding, for sixty kids, in five-gallon buckets every day. It is even harder to dry clothes and bedding for sixty kids every day, especially during the rainy season. Electricity is expensive. Dryers donated by Samaritans Purse took two years to hook up and are run sparingly due to the high operating expense.

Sanitation. Sixty kids go to the bathroom a lot. Toilet paper is hard to come by, and the expense of toilet paper adds up when multiplied by the daily needs of each child. Diapers, cloth or disposable, are expensive and even harder to come by and are needed both day and night. Sixty kids have a lot of runny noses, and Kleenex does not exist. Maintaining a clean living and playing area can be tricky. Antibacterial soap is an extreme luxury, and clean hand towels, paper or cloth, barely exist. Germ management in a third world orphanage is a very real and expensive challenge.

Under these conditions, the Welcome Home staff does a respectable job of maintaining the facilities. The improved general health of the children reflects that their efforts are paying off. Since Mandy has implemented rigorous standards toward better hygiene and has trained an employee to serve as a practical nurse, the number of deaths at the home has decreased from five to ten per month to less than one per year. Nonetheless, effective germ management practice requires resources. Supporters who choose to invest in this worthwhile cause provide a daily blessing to both children and staff.

Phone Calls Home—Like a Breath of Fresh Air

Tonight's phone call home was like a cool breeze after a long, hot, and steamy day; it was pure refreshment! We have been waiting for our court date for days and days now. The initial excitement and adventure of the trip is wearing off, and I'm feeling a heart-sick longing for home. Hearing the children's voices brought to mind a stream of memories; their smiles, hugs, and giggles. Not knowing when we are going to get our court date or how the ongoing delay might affect our anticipated timeframe for returning home, I am beginning to feel my heart being torn. We need to return home to Wisconsin as soon as possible, but we cannot leave without Rhoda and Maria. Prayerfully, all will come together so we can return home together within the allotted timeframe. Uncertainty can be very stressful.

Chapter 6

Visa Photos

While we waited for our court appointment, we took care of several other important tasks. One of those was obtaining the necessary photos for the girls' visas. Joseph had taken Rhoda and Maria into town prior to our arrival to have their pictures taken. On our first Monday in Jinja, Joseph took us to the photo shop to pick up the packet of visa pictures. They were cut and stacked nicely and placed in a paper sleeve to keep them together. I removed the photos from the sleeve to see how they turned out, and while the pictures were clear, Rhoda and Maria look scared to death. Oh well, these pictures would have to do.

When we returned to our room that evening, I read through our immigration document requirements to make sure we had enough copies of the photos for our purposes. As I read, I discovered that these pictures were not the proper size as required by the USCIS for the Exit Visas. The next day we had to ask Joseph to take us back to the photo shop to repeat the process, this time for slightly larger pictures. When we returned to pick up the new photos, they still looked like mug shots, but at least they were the right size. I decided to put both the small and large pictures in my document folder. Having both sets of photos, each sized differently, would prove to be an unexpected blessing.

Encountering Life in Uganda

Our accommodations in Jinja were at a place called Ling Ling. Before we arrived, we both thought the name sounded Chinese. As it turned out, it was Chinese. The owner of Ling Ling had come to Uganda years before to work on a public works project. This man had led an amazing life. He had grown up in poverty in rural China. Because of limited access to resources, he didn't have an opportunity to go to college, but he knew that he needed education to have a chance in life. So he spent three years teaching himself English. He managed to pass an English competency exam, which enabled him to gain employment in public works construction. When China won a contract with the Ugandan government, his English speaking abilities earned him a place on the project (China has a strong and growing presence throughout Africa). He spent several years working in Uganda, and then the Tiananmen Square event occurred. He had no desire to return to China and applied for asylum in both the United States and Uganda. Both countries granted asylum to him, but only Uganda granted asylum to his wife. Rather than take the risk of never getting approval for his wife to join him in the United States, he chose to stay in Uganda. Since that time, he had become a successful businessman. To be successful, however, he had to completely remake himself. He took cooking classes to learn how to make Chinese food, opened a Chinese restaurant (Ling Ling), and bought an old, colonial-style residence. He and his family lived upstairs, and he converted the downstairs into an inn. Mark and I have the utmost respect for this hard working man.

We have fond memories of our stay at Ling Ling, but it was not without its challenges. First, in the heat and extreme humidity, air conditioning was a luxury we had to do without. Second, dusk brought with it the mosquito hour. The accommodations were far from air tight, and the mosquitoes, and the occasional Gecko, would easily find their way into our room. While we had received preventative inoculations for malaria, we still attempted to minimize our exposure by sleeping underneath the large mosquito netting that hung from the ceiling. This kept the mosquitoes away, but it also cut down on air circulation while we slept.

Ling Ling had running water and electricity; however, the aging pipes meant that the toilet leaked sewage water. A bowl had been placed underneath the leaking pipe that led out of the toilet. Being the kind person he is, Mark willingly dumped the sewage from the bowl daily.

Uganda had electric power generating capabilities, but the electricity was also sold to other countries in the region. This meant that the power would go out most nights, sometimes as early as 7:00 p.m., and would typically remain out for about four hours. During these periods, we had no light (other than a few candles provided by Ling Ling), and no fan, which at least provided some reprieve from the heat. Without the fan, I felt as if I was literally roasting underneath the mosquito netting. On most nights, the heat was too much and I just couldn't sleep, so I would read my book or write in my journal, all the while sweating until the electricity resumed and the fan turned back on. I am definitely a northern girl.

The power outages led to at least one interesting incident. One evening after returning from the orphanage, Mark and I were hungry. Previously, we had purchased some food from the local market, which we kept in bags in our suitcase to keep the critters away. One of the food items was a loaf of bread. Now, in Uganda, rather than using ties to keep plastic bread bags secure, they tie a knot at the end of the bag. Often, there is a tiny pinhole opening at the knot end of the bag. When we returned home that night, the power was out and it was difficult to see. Using our headlamps conservatively, we set up our tuna sandwiches in very dim light and ate in the dark. About halfway through my sandwich, I recalled having seen a few very tiny ants at the knot on the bread bag when I was in the food suitcase earlier that morning. Running the image of those few ants to its logical conclusion, I decided to flip on my headlamp and look at my sandwich. Startled, I yelled, "Ants!" My sandwich was saturated with hundreds, maybe thousands, of tiny ants. The bread looked as if it was in motion! I immediately spit out what was in my mouth and threw the remaining half of my sandwich in the garbage. As I did this, I looked over at Mark, who had nearly finished eating his sandwich. Rather than spit it out, he shrugged his shoulders, swallowed, and popped the last bit of his sandwich into his mouth. He figured one more bite couldn't do any more harm. Exactly what diseases can one contract from eating tiny African ants? We have no idea. Other than needing Immodium AD for a couple of days, we seemed to be OK.

Our many trips walking the mile back and forth between Ling Ling and the orphanage revealed a great deal about life in Uganda. We enjoyed listening to what I called the "tree band," which met almost every evening in a large open field to the west of the road. The field had one lone tree in the middle of it where six to ten people gathered in the evening to play their band instruments. I remember hearing a tuba, a couple of trumpets, a saxophone, maybe a clarinet, and a big bass drum. While it seemed so out of place to see and hear that creative expression in that environment, it was refreshing to hear them play, like an oasis. It was literally music to our ears.

At the top of the hill on the outskirts of town, we always encountered an unavoidable stench. An industrial-sized garbage container was located on the street corner. In principle, having a garbage container in the neighborhood seemed like a good idea. However, the resources were not available to dump the container, so after a while the garbage just piled up. To make more room in the container, an attempt was made to burn the garbage. Unfortunately, the refuse didn't actually burn. It just turned into a smoldering mess that lasted for days. The mix of rotten garbage and smoldering smoke would make me gag. Every day, as we approached that particular corner, Mark and I would look at each other, pick up the pace, and hold our breath as best we could. The folks in the neighborhood, however, didn't seem to react to the mess or the smell. Since they had probably never seen garbage handled in any other way, this unpleasant circumstance may not have been considered a significant problem. Given a myriad of other challenges and limited resources, resolving the garbage issue was likely not the highest priority. I certainly came to appreciate the value of the excellent infrastructure throughout the United States. I know many people complain about the challenges with maintaining infrastructure and core services in the U.S., but a short visit in a place that is truly lacking would certainly result in a change of perspective.

One of our most memorable encounters was with a man named Mirembe. His name, which means peace, was very fitting. Mirembe was very lean, medium height, light framed, and muscular. From a distance, judging by his physique, I would guess that he was in his thirties. But as we approached him and looked at his face, we realized that he was actually much older. While we never knew exactly how old he was, our best guess was that he was in his sixties. One reason Mirembe was in such good physical condition was because his job required hard labor: Mirembe was the sole worker charged with the task of digging a three-foot-deep by two-foot-wide ditch along the road between Ling Ling and the orphanage, a distance of one mile. His only tools were a shovel and a pick. Mark respected Mirembe's diligence in that hard and dirty work, because in his earlier years he had also worked as a manual laborer shoveling off layers of roofing material. Considering the difficult life that Mirembe led, it's easy to imagine that he might have become hard and calloused. He was just the opposite: kind, gentle, and peaceful. While he was steady in his work, he welcomed the opportunity to talk with us now and then. Most of our discussions were composed primarily of small talk, but embedded in our conversations were some very meaningful nuggets, at least for us. When he saw us with the two girls, he noted that he thought it was a good thing to help the children—there were so many in need.

During one conversation, Mark told Mirembe that he appreciated how hard he worked.

Mirembe shrugged and responded, "I am hungry. Therefore, I work." Then he paused and said, "But I do not have anything else to do anyway."

Mark nodded, thought for a moment, and then said, "I suppose we all must work in order to eat."

Mirembe insightfully responded, "Yes, but I think it is a little different for me than you."

Contrasting Mirembe's digging job with teaching a course at the university, Mark replied, "Yes. I suppose that is true." Mirembe's simple wisdom hit us squarely.

During one of our waiting days, Mandy asked Joseph to take us to see the Bujagali Falls. This is a gorgeous section of the Nile River famous for its challenging class III, IV, and even V rapids. While we were there enjoying the view, a kayaker carefully negotiated his way down the rapids. He did a masterful job getting through the challenging falls upright. The kayaker was followed by what the locals call a "Bujagali Swimmer." These swimmers are typically young men from a nearby village who make their living by entertaining tourists. For 5,000 shillings (about $2.50), the swimmer jumps into the raging river with only a yellow jerry can. A jerry can is a plastic five-gallon container typically used for carrying drinking water. This buoyant, flimsy jug is the swimmer's only lifeline, helping him stay afloat as he makes his way through the harshest part of the rapids. After seeing the swimmer accomplish this dangerous feat, I concluded that I didn't want to support this type of industry. The risk to the swimmer's life was very real. I appreciated the fact that he wanted and needed to earn an income, but was it worth it? When the lean and muscular swimmer we had observed returned from his ride, I couldn't help but notice his eyes. They were very cloudy, and it appeared that he was partially blind. Perhaps his vision was so limited that this was his best source of income. Nevertheless, it seemed like an extreme way to make a living.

The Goodbye Party

After spending most of the first weekend together, Rhoda and Maria transitioned from sleeping at the orphanage to staying with us full-time at Ling Ling. They were beginning to understand that their home was about to change. We used the pictures in a book we had made about our family to explain that we would be going home to Wisconsin where we would reunite with Jack, A.J., and Megan. In an effort to bring closure to their Welcome Home days, we set a date to throw a goodbye party.

We worked with Ozzie's restaurant to set up a party for thirty two- and three-year-old children plus about ten staff. We wanted to serve sausages, chips, ice cream, and punch. Back in the United States, we would have referred to these menu items as hot dogs, French fries, ice cream, and juice.

Jude, the owner of the restaurant, was an older Australian woman who was a fellow Christian. For many years she had lived in Jinja and run the small restaurant serving primarily foreigners. Traditional egg, meat, and toast breakfasts, hamburgers, and fish and chips were served with safe food handling practices. Being missionary minded, she used the small restaurant as her own outreach ministry, bringing in at-risk teenagers to train as cooks and servers. There were a couple of teenage girls with whom she had become very close over time. Though she never formally adopted these kids, she loved them, brought them into her home, and raised them as her own. She once told us that her own children back home often pleaded with her to return to Australia, where she could live a more comfortable life. Mark asked her whether she would ever go back. As she stood there, in what appeared to be semi-disrepair with teeth in need of care and back hunched over, she shook her head. Life was real in Uganda. The needs around her were so great; she felt she could do something useful. Why go back and live the life of a retiree, waiting to die? No, she planned to keel over someday while running her small shop in Jinja, Uganda.

We weren't sure when the court proceedings were going to be completed, but we decided to go ahead with the party as we were spending less and less time each day interacting with the children and staff at Welcome Home. On the day of the party, the four of us walked up to the orphanage at 3:30 p.m. to meet everyone. When we arrived, we could see that this was a big occasion for the older kids at the orphanage. Everyone was freshly bathed and dressed in what appeared to be brand new clothes. All of the older children piled into the Welcome Home van and Joseph's SUV. I also rode in the van. I think I counted twenty-three children and adults squished into the typical twelve-passenger van. I was completely engulfed with the happy sounds of children singing at the top of their lungs. They actually sounded very good with the mums singing harmony in the background. I appreciated the joy filled music that poured out of their hearts. I even made a note to buy some *Cedarmont Praise and Worship* CD's for our van rides when we got home. Hopefully, the happy sounds would help Rhoda and Maria feel right at home when we arrived back in Wisconsin.

We arrived at Ozzie's and arranged the children into two straight lines. As with any group of young children, this was a lot like herding cats. For some reason, I remember Johnny so clearly in this scene. He looked so handsome wearing a yellow and navy blue shirt with navy blue shorts and sandals. He looked much older than many of the children and his eyes sparkled. His smile was especially beautiful as he cheerfully tried to get the other children around him to stand still in line. He was a natural leader with a gentle charisma. Whenever we were around the larger group of children, I spent my time watching Johnny. I would look for opportunities to play with him, hug him, and connect with him in any real way possible. I wanted him to know that he was special. Johnny and I both knew that we were there to bring only Rhoda and Maria home with us. Without the use of words between us, I somehow wanted him to know that I cared for him too.

We waited in our lines until Jude waved us into her open-air, porch-like shop. As the children filed in, they were seated at the tables in orderly rows. Considering how many children there were in the shop, they behaved fairly well. They ate their sausages, spilled...I mean drank their punch, and gobbled up their chips. By the time the ice cream was served, their bellies were getting full. Some managed to empty their cups of the cold dessert, while others were not used to eating such sweet treats. Between the bright red punch and the ice cream, I was sure that some of the children would end up with tummy aches.

Though we knew this wasn't the last time we would actually see everyone from the orphanage, Joseph, Mark, Rhoda, Maria, and I stayed back in the shop while the other children piled back into the Welcome Home van. Watching their friends leave, Rhoda and Maria stood at the top of the stairs waving and yelling goodbye to all the people they loved. All I could think was, *I am so thankful they are so happy to be coming home with us.*

When it did come time to say goodbye to everyone from Welcome Home for the last time, I went to find Johnny. Most of the staff and children were huddled around Rhoda and Maria, saying their final goodbyes. But Johnny was on the front lawn by himself, looking down at the dirt cloud he had kicked up with his feet. I knelt down in front of him, reached out, and held his hand. As I tried to look him in the eye, I said, "Goodbye Johnny. I sure will miss you." Johnny kept looking at the ground. He slowly pulled his hand out of mine, turned, and walked away. He couldn't look at me that one last time. I don't know if it was a meaningful moment in his life, but it certainly was in mine. I left part of my heart back in Uganda with Johnny. I often wonder if providence will weave his path back together with ours at some point in the future.

Phone Calls Home—Many Smiles

Tonight's phone call home was filled with many smiles. Now that we've been gone almost two weeks, I've been feeling guilty that my mom has had such a demanding role and has had to sacrifice so much in support of our family's expansion. Thankfully, her stories tonight brought me a much different perspective. She talked about the kids endearingly and told some animated tale about each one of them. It was a great relief to hear her say she was so thankful to have this extended time with the kids by herself; that it enabled her to experience their delightful personalities in a way that a normal visit, especially with Mark and I around, could never provide. I feel blessed to know that my mom is not only surviving, she is actually enjoying this experience. Thank you, God.

This is the picture that was hanging on my sister's bulletin board that drew us in with the question, "What about you?"

Together at last

Bonding with Mark after he gave them each a shoulder ride down the soccer field

A special hug from Rhoda's primary daytime Mum at Welcome Home

Johnny's smile and gentle charisma won our hearts too

Five kids six and under!

Adoption Day in April 2006 at the Walworth County Court House

A thriving Rhoda and Maria April 2009

Summer 2010 - the cousins from the Kenny side of the family (Front Row: Seth 5, Megan 6, Maria 7, A.J. 8, Rhoda 7; Middle Row: Jack 10, Joshua 11, Grandpa and Grandma Kenny, Kailyn 17, Luke 3; Back Row: Alissa 16, Christian 13, Matthew 18

Our family today playing at the Sleeping Bear Sand Dunes in Empire, Michigan

Chapter 7

The High Court

As we stayed in Jinja, we gained a new perspective of the world, developed new friendships, and strengthened our bond with the girls. Nevertheless, the delays were troubling. Things were not progressing as quickly as we had anticipated. When we arrived in Uganda on January 6, we expected to be in court that same day. Instead we had to wait through the weekend, hoping that Monday would be the day we would see the judge. Unfortunately, all we heard from the lawyer on Monday was, "Maybe tomorrow."

Finally, on January 10, David called to tell us that we had a court appointment the next day. He explained that due to our time constraints and the unavailability of his preferred judge, he had reluctantly made arrangements with a different, more conservative judge. We were relieved to have our court hearing set and anticipated being finished with the official court procedures by the afternoon of the court date or the following day at the latest, if all went well.

The Judge

At last, it was our day to go to the High Court in Kampala. We woke up early in the morning and packed all our bags, expecting that we would not be returning to Welcome Home again. We made the two-hour drive to Kampala. While the mood prior to the appointment was tense, Mark and I were optimistic. We were looking forward to getting through this hoop. After sitting on the hard wooden chairs in the open-air waiting area for some time, we were finally called before Justice Eldad Mwangusya.

The honorable judge, who was tall, broad, and imposing, invited David to explain the circumstances of this particular adoption case. David was dressed sharply in his navy blue, pinstripe suit and exuded confidence. He explained that we were requesting that our adoption be exempt from the normal three-year waiting period. Apparently, Ugandan law only allows exceptions to this rule in cases where the child has need of special consideration, typically medically related. David argued that any case involving a child without a family to care for him or her should be deemed a special case. As the judge listened, his expression became increasingly intense. His eyes narrowed and his forehead furrowed. The judge was clearly annoyed. He cut David off mid-sentence with his booming voice, "Why are you bringing this request to my court? You know what the law says, and this is clearly not a special case."

David attempted one more plea, but the judge abruptly dismissed us, indicating that he would make his ruling shortly. It didn't take deep thinking to recognize that approval of our request to adopt Rhoda and Maria was very unlikely. Nonetheless, we had to wait for the ruling.

While we waited, Mark and I finally had a chance to read what the law actually said, and we understood the judge's concern. The law specifies that children may not be adopted without first completing a three-year probationary period, no exceptions. In fact, the Ugandan courts had never permitted the adoption of a healthy child to a foreigner without first requiring the probationary period—the children were to remain in Uganda for the entire three-year period. This law was in place for good reason as there were stories of Ugandan orphans being "adopted" by foreigners only to be trained as servants or slaves. Unfortunately, human trafficking is still a reality in Africa and orphans are particularly vulnerable to exploitation. The courts, however, sometimes granted adoptions of children with special needs. In our case, Rhoda would have fallen into the special needs category, but Maria was very healthy despite having been born prematurely.

We learned that our lawyer had decided to proceed with the request for both girls as healthy adoptions. We were to be a test case: If our request was approved, the precedent would be set, and this could potentially open the door for many more international adoptions. While there was much potential good that could result from enabling more families from outside the country to adopt orphans, there was also a danger. International adoptions can generate profits for a number of parties, including the lawyers who process adoptions and the newspapers that charge exorbitant fees to foreigners to post simple classified advertisements. In some cases, it was said that desperate young moms would even sell their babies for cash. There was also a concern that some women would voluntarily become pregnant with the intention of selling the babies into the international adoption market. International adoptions, if not properly monitored, could be a very messy business.

In any case, David had hoped to open this door, and he had planned to do so by working with a judge who was known to interpret the law liberally. It turned out that our court appointment delay was due to the fact that this particular judge had recently been charged with allegations of corruption and had left the country. Finally, realizing that the lenient judge would not be returning any time soon, David had decided to move ahead with the court proceedings with this other judge.

As we left the judge's chambers I was furious, whereas Mark, though clearly agitated by the hearing, was far more composed. We had come all this way to adopt these two beautiful girls, and our lawyer did not discuss the options we had and the risks associated with each course of action. After waiting a number of days for our hearing, this outcome put us in a very vulnerable situation. It was likely that we would not be able to adopt Rhoda and Maria within the Ugandan courts.

As the day wore on, we waited away the afternoon in the blazing hot sun on the grassy yard of the High Court. We hoped the ruling would come before the close of the business day, but it did not. Reluctantly, we made the two-hour trip back to Jinja and checked back into our same room at Ling Ling. All the next day, we waited for the cell phone to ring to call us back to the high court. The call did not come because the ruling had not come.

Finally, on the third day, the judge called for us. David attempted to make one more plea, but the judge stopped him and issued his ruling: Our case did not warrant exemption from the law; the court would not grant adoption.

At this point, I was ready to explode but Mark's steady nature proved invaluable. He requested permission to speak, and it was granted. He asked, "If the court is unwilling to grant adoption, may we request irrevocable legal guardianship?"

We had learned that in some cases, the courts had granted this "Irrevocable Legal Guardianship" to foreigners. In our case, irrevocable guardianship would allow us to return home with the children, and then adopt them through the U.S. courts.

The judge indicated that it was possible, but the request would require a whole new set of documents and another proceeding. The door was not completely closed on the possibility of bringing the girls home with us, but who knew how long it would take to draw up the new documents and set another court date?

As the judge spoke again, our hearts sank. He told us that his time in court over the next couple of weeks would be limited as he was in ill health and was scheduled to leave the country to seek medical attention. I knew that this was the only judge currently serving the court, and I felt a surge of panic. I too requested permission to speak.

Seeking mercy from the judge I said, "Your honor, please know that in addition to these two girls before you, we also have three young children back in Wisconsin who are six, three, and one. We are already scheduled to be away for twenty-one days, so any delay will be very hard on all of us, including my mother who is caring for our other children."

With tears streaming down my cheeks, I left the judge's chambers hoping that his heart would be softened toward us. I wanted him to understand that we were as upset with our lawyer as he was. I felt angry at David and powerless to bring a quick resolution to this crisis. Would we have to leave the girls behind? Would Mark have to return home on his own and leave me to continue this struggle with the court? Or would I return home to be reunited with the kids and leave Mark behind? Our time was running out.

From the Bowels

During our visits to the High Court, when we weren't meeting in the judge's chamber, we waited. We did a lot of waiting. During the idle times, we would typically sit on the lawn outside the High Court. On one of these occasions, Maria told us she had to go to the bathroom. This seemingly simple task turned out to be a major experience.

Rhoda and Maria were mostly potty trained, but we still had them wear pull-ups just in case of accidents. The whole court process included getting up very early, long car rides, and sitting still and quiet for long periods of time. This was pretty hard on the girls, and the pull-ups helped ease the stress. If either of them did need to go, they would typically call out "su su" or "ka ka" and off we would run to the toilet. In addition, the girls had chronic diarrhea, a symptom of the intestinal parasites they carried.

The open-air courthouse complex contained only one small women's bathroom with two stalls, located up three flights of stairs. It was very dirty, the faucet barely worked, lighting failed to reach the toilet stalls, a coat hanger was rigged up to flush one toilet, and only one of the toilet stalls had a door, which contained a sizable hole where the missing handle should have been. Regardless of its condition, I was very thankful to have a bathroom where I could take Maria.

Maria went into the stall without the door, hopped up on to the toilet, and started to take care of business. So far so good! After a few tinkles, I asked her if she was done, but she shook her head, "no."

As I waited, a few ladies came in and used the other stall. I smiled as they passed by with a look of inquiry: *Why is this muzungu (white foreigner) with this African child?*

Maria continued to sit on the toilet a while longer, and then she began to cry.

"Are you done?" I asked.

She shook her head, "no."

"Are you ok?"

Maria didn't respond. Our ability to communicate was very limited at this point. We had the words for "bathroom," "food," "drink," and "be quiet" worked out, but all other communication required charades. After fifteen minutes on the toilet with the last five in tears, I began to wonder whether her legs were beginning to fall asleep from sitting for so long. I tried to help her off the toilet, but she cried all the more.

I asked her if she needed to go "ka ka" and she nodded, "Yes!" I then asked her if she wanted to sit back on the toilet. She nodded, "YES!" So I helped her back up on the toilet.

A little worried, I began to review her diet since she last went "ka ka." We had been traveling in the car a lot. Maybe she had not had enough water. Perhaps those shortbread cookies that she typically ate while riding in the car were beginning to slow her bowels down.

Regardless of the cause, this girl began to wail! In this open-air complex, her crying was definitely heard all over. What to do? What to do? I thought, "Maybe if I stand her up on some paper and let her go on the ground, it will be easier for her because she is used to a going on a child-sized squat pot at the orphanage."

I looked out the bathroom door to see if Mark was out there. Mark wasn't there, but the security guard happened to be passing by. He looked at me and asked, "Is something wrong?"

I shook my head no, explaining that she just had to go "ka ka" and was having a bit of trouble. He gave me a stern look that said, "Please keep her quiet as everyone in this entire facility can hear her!"

Have you ever been in one of those circumstances where things go from bad to worse, and there is absolutely nothing you can do? I was in that exact situation. Maria was in an all out panic and started to scream!

I looked out the window to see if Mark and Joseph were aware of my dilemma. They were. I could see them looking up at the bathroom window and apparently talking to each other about the noise.

I went back to Maria and decided that the drop paper method was not working, so I set her back up on the toilet. All the while, the screaming continued. Another woman came into the bathroom and asked me what was wrong with the child. I told her my theory: I thought she was used to having loose "ka ka" and that perhaps she was feeling a pressure on her bottom that she doesn't ordinarily feel when she has a bowel movement. She gave me a look that said "yeah right," and then left the bathroom.

I started to consider the options for resolving this emergency: 1) wait it out with the screaming, or 2) put Maria's clothes back on and drag her out of the building all the while screaming her head off. Either way, the entire open-air complex would be blanketed with the panic of this screaming two-year-old girl. If she was able to accomplish her goal, at least she would stop screaming.

I decided to stay and wait it out. I went into the toilet stall with her to coach her on pushing. I reassured her that it would be ok, and then I encouraged her to PUSH. I thought to myself, *For as loud as she is screaming, this pooper must be as hard as a rock!*

We endured a few more minutes of hysterics and finally, SUCCESS! I look into the toilet expecting to see something worthy of forty minutes of crying and screaming; instead I saw a very normal-sized pooper.

I think she went crazy because she was so used to having chronic diarrhea. Feeling the normal pressure of a regular stool alarmed her. Oh my. I hoped that wasn't indicative of the coming months, given that we would be getting her intestinal system cleaned up.

The Court Order

When our second long court day was finally over, David indicated that his office would immediately prepare another set of documents, this time to request Irrevocable Legal Guardianship. If the judge was available and our request was granted, we could still bring the girls home and then later adopt them through the U.S. courts. This was our only option—the option we would have pursued initially if we had fully understood what the law said in the first place.

I was still steaming with frustration from our last court appearance. I wanted to lay into David and make sure he knew that his strategy had put us in an extremely vulnerable position. We had not volunteered to be guinea pigs.

We can only guess about David's motivation in handling our case the way he did. It's not possible to see his heart. Maybe he wanted to open the door to more international adoptions because the need was so great and so many children could be helped. Or perhaps he hoped to profit financially from the influx of business that might come with a flood of new international adoptions. Regardless of David's motivations, we had to move forward—we needed him.

By Monday, January 16, David had prepared the new guardianship documents and submitted them to the courts for the judge to review prior to our next appointment. We stayed in Jinja while we waited for David to call us back to Kampala for our new court hearing, hoping that the call would come early in the week. We were completely at the mercy of the judge, who had spent a long weekend out of the country pursuing medical care for his illness. We prayed and tried to maintain our composure while we waited and watched as our window of time closed in with every passing day.

Finally, on Thursday, the judge called for us to come to his chambers. We were all very tense and anxious. To our great relief, the hearing was brief, and the judge ruled that we would be granted Irrevocable Legal Guardianship for Rhoda and Maria. Finally, thirteen days later than we had originally anticipated, we had the answer were hoping for: We would be able to take the girls home! All we needed now were the official documents in our hands. To satisfy the requirements of the U.S. Embassy, we had to have a Court Order from the Ugandan courts, stating that they understood that we would be returning to the United States and filing for adoption in the U.S. courts. The judge agreed to write that in the ruling. With any luck we would have the documents by 2:00 p.m.

The Orphan Investigation

We were sitting outside the High Court in the blazing hot sun on the crisp, dried lawn waiting for the paperwork, when the cell phone rang. It was Nathan Flook from the U.S. Embassy in Kampala. He informed us that his staff at the embassy would need to do a more extensive orphan investigation on Rhoda. He was not at liberty to say what was in question, but he did say this could take anywhere from a couple of days to two weeks. I couldn't believe what I had just heard! Why would there be questions about Rhoda's background? More was known about her story than Maria's, so we had not anticipated any inquiry regarding her background.

Questions raced through my mind. Why was Nathan just now getting around to this investigation? We had been in the country for almost two weeks already, why didn't he start the investigation earlier? Just when I thought we were free to leave Uganda, we had another obstacle cross our path that was completely out of our control. Why did this keep happening?

We called Mandy Sydo to ask if she had encountered this situation with any of the other adoptions. Mainly, I wanted to know how long this would really take, and I wanted a shoulder to cry on. Mandy told us she had not dealt with many in-depth orphan investigations, but she reassured us that the story on Rhoda's background was accurate and on record at Welcome Home. In addition, she encouraged us to call Mr. Flook and suggest that he call the missionary couple who found Rhoda. I had their phone number with me, so it was easy to pass along. Mandy also reassured us that she was praying for a quick and favorable outcome of the investigation.

I was beginning to grow weary. I wanted to go home. I wanted to go home **within our allotted timeframe,** and I wanted to go home **with** Rhoda and Maria. I couldn't bear the thought of leaving without them, but I missed the other three kids terribly. I also couldn't bear the thought of waiting in Uganda for another two weeks for the orphan investigation.

Typically, when I am faced with a roadblock, I am persistent in finding another way to get through. But on that day, I could see no way around, no alternative routes, no contacts who could help us circumvent the process. Once again all we could do was wait. I found comfort in Mandy's reminder that she had a team of prayer warriors from her home church intervening on our behalf. This reassurance calmed me considerably as fervent prayer had been effective in repeatedly clearing paths in my life. I'm not the best at "walking by faith," but at this time I considered the occasions when I saw God's hand at work. I decided to give the outcome back to God remembering that this was His plan in the first place. Mark and I just needed to pray, wait, and watch.

Shortly after our disheartening conversation with Mr. Flook, we received the notarized approval from the Ugandan court granting us Irrevocable Legal Guardianship of Rhoda and Maria. We were relieved to finally have the Court Order, but it was anti-climactic. We still couldn't leave the country until the orphan investigation was completed and the U.S. Embassy provided exit visas for Rhoda and Maria.

With approval from the court, we decided to stay at a hotel in Entebbe so that we would be close to the airport and ready to depart as soon as the paperwork from the U.S. Embassy in Kampala was completed. We knew that Mark would need to travel back to the embassy to get the papers, but he could use a taxi service when needed.

Our hearts were somber as Joseph drove us to the Entebbe Airport Hotel, but that mood quickly shifted to surprise and dismay as we pulled into the hotel driveway. It looked like a war zone! Walls were missing, piles of bricks lay everywhere, and rickety wooden scaffolding surrounded the outside walls of the hotel compound. It took me a moment to fully realize that the hotel was under construction. Our adventure wasn't over yet.

Joseph dropped the four of us off at the front entrance along with our pile of bags. Saying goodbye to Joseph was difficult. If things went as planned, we would not see him again. He had been so helpful and patient through the long process, and we had developed a close connection and friendship with him. Though it was difficult, we said our goodbyes and exchanged hugs, and off he went back to

Jinja. We would miss his support and the opportunity to further enjoy our new friendship.

Phone Calls Home—That Was Encouraging

I talked with my sister Elizabeth tonight, and our conversation was very encouraging. Before we left for Africa, she said that she would keep in contact with Mom to make sure she was holding up OK taking care of the babes. Yesterday, she made the two-hour trip to Whitewater to see Mom and the kids and help with baths and general clean up as needed. She was pleased to report that Mom was really holding up and that the kids all looked well-cared for, rested, and that the inner workings of the dynamics at home seemed calm and relaxed. Coping with being away for such a long time and dealing with so many glitches to our efforts here is <u>so</u> much more manageable when the phone calls home are filled with such encouraging reports. I am so thankful!

Chapter 8

Our Weekend in Purgatory (I mean Entebbe)

We were all feeling very travel weary when we arrived in Entebbe. We had originally planned to spend the weekend as tourists on a safari in Kenya. Instead, we were stuck in an open-air hotel that was under major construction. After we settled into our room, we decided to go down to the restaurant for a bite to eat. That night at supper, we learned an important lesson: Do not touch Maria's food once it is placed before her. As we ordered our meals, we decided that the girls could split a platter of the delicious looking fish and chips. We asked the server to deliver an extra plate with the meal. The server arrived and placed the food in front of Maria and the empty plate before Rhoda.

As I transferred the fish and chips to Rhoda's plate, Maria began to whimper. Then she began to cry. Then she began to wail uncontrollably. Regardless of our efforts to console her, she cried and screamed all the more. What happened? What was the big deal? After five minutes of trying to settle her and get her to eat her dinner, I finally had to take her back to the room where she continued to wail for the next thirty minutes. After this experience, we were very careful not to touch Maria's plate once it was given to her. In Maria's eyes, she had taken ownership of the food as it was placed before her. Any changes or food transfers had to be made before giving the plate to Maria. We can only guess that, having grown up in the orphanage environment, protection of her food was important to her. This was one of our first indications that Maria was very particular and fastidious. She liked things just so.

That would not be the only screaming episode of the evening. In fact, the girls screamed almost every day at nap time as well as at bedtime. As the evening progressed, they were fine as we played, looked at books, brushed teeth, etc. But once we said, "its bedtime," all hell broke loose. Both girls wailed as if their lives were about to end.

We had no idea why they screamed. They only wanted to be with us, and yet somehow every night we experienced the onslaught of screaming. There was little we could do. We tried everything—comforting, rocking, sternly warning "sitika" (be quiet in Lugandan), even having the girls stand up against a wall. Nothing worked. Back at Ling Ling, we'd had some privacy and a buffer between us and the other guests. At the hotel in Entebbe, there was no buffer. The courtyard and other open-air rooms were just outside our window. The room had walls and a door, but the two windows were only screened. The girls screamed for an hour that night. I even left the curtains open so people could see that I was just lying on the bed with my arms around the girls singing them lullabies. Perhaps it was just our imagination, but the next morning it felt as if the other guests were giving us suspicious and questioning looks, *What are you doing with those poor girls?*

To this day we are not sure why they screamed every night. The pattern would continue for months. Our best guess is that during the day, everything was OK. The girls were starting a new chapter with us as their mom and dad. All was well. But at bedtime, the uncertainty of what might happen tomorrow came to the forefront. Today was good, but what would happen tomorrow? Would tomorrow mean a return to the orphanage? How were they to know whether the new circumstances were permanent or only temporary?

Embracing the Moment

On Friday, we had a lazy start to the day. We enjoyed a relaxed breakfast in the hotel restaurant with the girls. I was thankful that we had been able to find safe food to eat at each of our stops along the way this whole trip. In an attempt to tap into the "secret of life" as seen by musician James Taylor, we tried to "enjoy the passage of time" that day. In the morning, we stayed out of the hot sun and found shaded spots with a breeze in which to hide. We colored pictures and read the few children's books that we'd brought with us. In the afternoon, we decided to take the girls for a walk to downtown Entebbe.

Downtown only consisted of a few shops, but they were decent-sized traditional Ugandan shops. We walked across the highway, and while it was only two lanes, we actually had to watch out for traffic. Back in Jinja, the streets were often void of cars but filled with bicycles and pedestrians instead. We made our way past a cow tied up near a busy intersection and a few goats that were looking a little scrawny. We decided to stop in one of the stores to look around. After exploring a bit, we were excited to find a working chest freezer holding ice-cream bars! I wondered whether Rhoda and Maria had ever eaten a chocolate-covered, ice-cream bar on a stick. We bought four frozen treats, took them outside, and sat on the front steps of the store to eat our snack. About sixty seconds into this ice-cream adventure, Mark and I realized this was probably not such a good idea. The hot sun quickly melted the treats. While Mark and I sucked our ice cream down, the girl's bars had turned into a sticky, chocolate-covered mess. Mark went back into the store and tracked down some baby wipes to help capture the pool.

While Mark was in the store, the cell phone rang. I answered the call. It was Mr. Flook again, and this time there was very good news. The U.S. Embassy had completed its orphan investigation, and Rhoda had been approved to travel. We were extremely relieved! The bad news was that it was too late in the day to go to the embassy to complete the final paperwork. That task would have to wait until Monday. Nevertheless, spending the weekend in Entebbe was going to be much easier now that we knew we had everything we needed. We were confident we would be traveling to Kenya on Monday.

The Zoo

On Saturday, we had some time to relax, so we decided to visit a nearby zoo. We arranged a taxi and off we went. The zoo had a number of large animals: lions, elephants, giraffes, zebras, monkeys, and the like. While it wasn't the Kenyan safari we had originally planned for the weekend, it seemed like a reasonable, though less exciting, alternative.

We worked our way through the zoo looking at all of the animals. The monkeys were the most dynamic, climbing and chattering in their authentic exhibit. The girls really liked the monkeys. Later, as we finished our walk through the zoo, we came to a children's play area. To our surprise, the very same monkeys that we thought were residing in a secured exhibit came running down the paths to the play area to "monkey" around! We were all intrigued—they came right up to us! The girls were both excited and afraid. They stood on top of the small slide and squealed something exciting to each other. They were speaking Lugandan, so we had no idea what was being said.

We needed that happy day playing at the zoo together. Though our bonding was going well, our days had been filled with too many stressful events. That was one of the most enjoyable outings we'd had together.

Sunday Church

During our time in Uganda, we had a chance to attend church on three occasions. On the first two Sundays, we experienced the more charismatic church that many of the mums and children from Welcome Home attended. These services were filled with singing and a lot of fervent-style preaching. Relative to our experience in the United States, the services were also very long—about three-and-a-half hours. We appreciated the opportunity to worship with our Ugandan brothers and sisters in Christ, but I have to admit that I was not used to the lengthy services. For me, the heat coupled with holding a child in my lap while sitting on a narrow wooden board that did not allow my feet to touch the ground was grueling. I remember thinking, *When will the service be over? Doesn't anyone have to go to the bathroom? Aren't they thirsty? What about lunch? How do they manage to happily sit on these narrow rough boards for three-and-a-half hours?*

Sitting in church that day, I came to a realization: In an environment where basic necessities (food, water, and bathroom facilities) are difficult to come by and creature comforts (reasonably comfortable chairs) are rare, people's physical needs simply are not at the forefront. In addition, in a society without distractions such as television, video games, and cars, the opportunity to participate in a faith community is a welcome privilege. I'm sure some would prefer an even longer service, thankful for the opportunity to be away from the small hut that many call home. Attempting to embrace this new perspective, I worked to appreciate this special opportunity and enjoy the experience. The breeze that occasionally found its way through the open-air windows provided some reprieve. The worship of the people was real. The joy I saw in their faces transcended their circumstances. I loved to watch one young boy, about twelve years old, lift his hands longingly as he sang praise to our Abba Father. It was evident that his hope was in the Lord.

When we arrived in Entebbe, I investigated nearby churches. We settled on a Catholic parish within walking distance of our hotel. The Catholic service was even longer than our previous two experiences—at least four hours. The homily was given by two church leaders and went on for hours. Though we couldn't understand what was being said, the speakers were apparently speaking English. If I really concentrated on listening, I could pick out about every fifth word. Eventually, my mind drifted from the message as I turned my attention to watching the people.

Mark and I were two of about six Caucasians in the church. We sat in the middle of a long row, being squeezed by bodies on both sides, as the church was packed. This church actually had solid walls and real windows, which meant that the only air movement came from a tiny oscillating fan about thirty-feet away. In short, there was no relief from the stifling heat. And there was no way we could discretely leave early or even take the girls to the bathroom. Interestingly, though the service was Catholic and very long, the

Eucharist was not celebrated. I'm guessing that the two men giving the homily were not ordained priests. Had it just been Mark and me, the heat and service length might have been tolerable. But with the girls sitting on our laps for hours, it was literally painful! Thankfully, Rhoda and Maria fell asleep about two hours into the service. This allowed me to focus on myself, trying to stay calm as feelings of claustrophobia overwhelmed me. When the service finally ended, we walked out, greatly relieved, but dripping with sweat.

We were becoming used to the sweat at that point. It was always refreshing to take a nice, cool shower in the early morning. With any luck, we would be sweat-free for about an hour. As soon as we started moving, the heat and humidity would kick in, and perspiration was unavoidable. That's just the way it was. We sort of grew accustomed to it after awhile. These experiences made me more thankful for our more comfortable church services back home. At the same time, they also gave me a fuller appreciation of how Christ is celebrated all around the world.

Time and Chance

"And I have seen something else under the sun:
The race is not to the swift or the battle to the
strong, nor does food come to the wise or wealth to
the brilliant or favor to the learned; but time and
chance happen to them all." -Ecclesiastes 9:11 NIV

Monday finally arrived, and we were ready for another full day. The plan was for me to stay with the girls in Entebbe, while Mark returned to Kampala to complete the approval process at the U.S. Embassy. If Mark was delayed for any reason, I would fly with the girls to Nairobi on my own. With the orphan investigation cleared and the irrevocable legal guardianship granted, we were allowed to take the girls out of Uganda, but we could not leave Kenya to return to the United States without the necessary documents from the U.S. Embassy in Kampala.

It was important for us to get the girls to Nairobi as soon as possible in order to proceed with their immigration physicals. I had no desire to go on alone to Nairobi. It was known to be a dangerous city, and managing the luggage and the girls would be overwhelming. We prayed that Mark would be able to successfully negotiate the remaining details in Kampala so that we could all fly to Nairobi together that evening. I made reservations with the hotel shuttle for the girls and me to be dropped off at the airport at 5:30 p.m.

The taxi driver who had taken us to the zoo was set to take Mark to Kampala very early in the morning. In Uganda, taxi services appear to be unregulated, so anyone can take up the business in just about any type of vehicle. In our case, the taxi driver had an old, rusty Toyota Corolla. In fact, most of the cars in Uganda were older used cars that the Japanese no longer wanted. Uganda was an excellent secondary market for such vehicles. Older cars, no longer marketable in Japan, were packed in large containers and shipped to Africa. Some of these vehicles were still quite nice, but the strict Japanese emissions standards forced the "retirement" of decent vehicles after only four years or so of use. This much older Corolla, however, had little left in its useful life, but it served the man who drove it by helping him earn a living. To avoid an exorbitant taxi fare, Mark had prearranged a deal with the taxi driver for the trip to Kampala. The man was happy for the business. He and his car would stay in Kampala and, if necessary, wait for Mark all day. I would stay back at the hotel with girls to complete the packing and prepare for our departure.

Mark left the room very early in the morning for a quick breakfast and then returned. It was 6:30 a.m., and as he was preparing to leave for the taxi the cell phone unexpectedly rang. It was Joseph. He was in a major panic! We had come to know Joseph pretty well, and this was very much out of character for him.

When Mark asked what happened, Joseph burst out, "I've been robbed!"

Apparently, he had been given a large amount of money to put in the safe, but it had been stolen before it could be secured. Joseph was greatly distressed because he knew how devastating this loss would be for the orphanage. Mark reassured Joseph, saying that even though the loss was great, the money was replaceable. Rather, it was Joseph who was irreplaceable. The orphanage, the children, and his family all needed him. God had put him there for a reason.

Finally, Mark said, "Joseph I must go to the embassy now, but everything will work out. We will find a way through this. Mandy will be disappointed, but she is a good woman. It will be OK."

Later we learned that while Mandy was understandably upset, she was generous in extending God's grace to Joseph. He learned a painful lesson and was deeply appreciative of Mandy as he was not dismissed from his job. We were greatly relieved to know that both Joseph and the orphanage were resilient and survived the crisis.

Anxious Hours of Waiting

Mark proceeded on his way to Kampala in the old Toyota Corolla that was doing its best to chug-a-long. The car moved pretty well going downhill, but it struggled to make it up hills. They arrived at the U.S. Embassy at about 8:00 a.m. As agreed, the taxi driver waited for Mark. Obtaining the approvals shouldn't take too long.

Mark made his way into the embassy and was able to meet with Nathan Flook, the lead representative who had been overseeing our case from the beginning. As Mr. Flook reviewed the documents, he noticed that we had the "Court Order" but not the necessary "Court Ruling." Was there a difference? We thought we had received all of the final documents from the court on Thursday. Mark quickly rifled through the three-inch-thick folder containing all of our official papers. We did not have a Court Ruling!

Mark left the embassy and immediately called our lawyer. David indicated that he could obtain a copy of the Court Ruling from the High Court and have it delivered to the embassy by noon. That seemed reasonable, so Mark settled in to wait outside the embassy.

Noon came and went, but the document did not arrive. At about 12:30 p.m., Mark called David to get an update. He didn't have any news to share and said he would check to see what was happening. In the meantime, Mark continued to wait outside the embassy. This time he called David every thirty minutes to check on the status of the document.

As it turned out, the judge was unavailable once again, and the court clerk could not be found. Without the judge or the clerk, the Court Ruling could not be prepared. David told Mark that he sent his assistant to the High Court to request the document, but nothing had been done yet.

By 2:30 p.m., Mark had run out of patience. He knew that he needed to be back in the U.S. Embassy by 3:30 p.m. so that Mr. Flook would have enough time to complete the final approvals. Still, no news came.

Mark called David yet again and implored him, "David, I do not want to send my wife to Nairobi alone. We paid you a lot of money to provide legal services. We need you now. You need to go to the High Court yourself and get the Court Ruling. You have more influence than your assistant."

David responded, "I am sorry, there is nothing I can do."

Any other person might have accepted this answer and headed home, but Mark had learned the value of persistence. His answer was succinct, "Just go down there, David!"

We have no idea what happened on the other end, but at 3:50 p.m., David's assistant called Mark to tell him that she was on her way…with the Court Ruling! Mark then called Mr. Flook to tell him that the document was coming and to request entrance to the embassy after the 4:00 p.m. closing time. Mr. Flook said he would allow entrance to the high-security building and that he would process the needed documents. The Court Ruling arrived at 4:10 p.m. Mark went into the embassy, obtained the needed approvals, and was out by 4:45 p.m. He ran off the embassy grounds and down the road to meet his taxi.

Mark jumped into the old Toyota and told the driver to hurry back to Entebbe. The driver didn't speak English very well, but he got the idea. He looked back at Mark and asked, "Fast?"

Mark replied, "Yes!"

The driver grinned and said, "OK."

Have you ever seen one of those fast car scenes in a movie where the car is swerving and weaving in and out of traffic, almost hitting vehicles coming in the opposite direction? Mark said his ride to the airport was just like that, only this was real life. The driver hauled full bore, weaving in and out of traffic. At one point, a large old delivery truck pulled out directly in front of the taxi. The taxi driver, with his gas pedal pressed to the floor, sharply cranked the steering wheel of the old Corolla, missing the truck by inches.

Meanwhile, back at the hotel, I had not heard from Mark. I knew that if everything had gone well, he would have been back by noon. As the clock closed in on 4:00 p.m., I asked God to clear the path for me and the girls and Mark. After praying (really it was more like begging and pleading with God), I decided it was time to close the suitcases, wake the girls from their nap, eat a snack, drink some water, and use the bathroom one last time. I didn't know what had happened to Mark, and so I decided to head to the airport with the girls on the 5:00 p.m. shuttle as planned. Wearing my backpack, I had to drag the two big roller suitcases and two strollers, with the girls each wearing a small backpack in tow. I taught them to walk behind me holding onto my backpack strap so that they could be close to me and at the same time allow my hands to be free to negotiate the hallway, lobby, and stairs with the bags.

We made it to the loading zone for the airport shuttle, but I still hadn't heard anything from Mark. While I was trying to stay calm, I was definitely feeling very stressed about leaving without him. Still, I went ahead to the airport with the girls, unloaded my mound of baggage, and managed to retrieve a luggage cart to move the baggage and the girls to the check-in counter. As I pushed the cart slowly toward the counter wondering how I was going to handle this trip all on my own, I heard a familiar, "Kate!" I turned to see Mark jumping out of the white taxi. Hallelujah! We would travel to Nairobi together, after all. God is not often early, but he is never late! Thank you, Lord.

Phone Calls Home—A Cool Drink of Water

I talked with Linda Brown today. She is watching the kids for the weekend so that my mom can make a trip home to attend the funeral of a close friend. Linda told me she was able to bring the kids with her to work on Friday and is keeping them at her home until Sunday night when my mom is scheduled to return.

Going into the phone call, I was feeling guilty that my children were actually being passed to her care for three days (having a contingency plan in place is one thing; actually having to use the contingency plan is another thing altogether.) I called to thank her for stepping in and to find out how everyone was doing. It sounded like she was completely comfortable bringing them into her routine. For Friday, she merely needed to leave fifteen minutes early to drop Jack off at school on her way into town. She then dropped A.J. and Megan off at the Children's Learning Center as she walked into her building.

She told me that the weekend had been "simply delightful." As a mother of five adult children, I guess having just three around was pretty easy. I know that when my kids sleep and eat well, they are typically a pretty manageable crew. Thankfully, they are also usually good sleepers, even in new environments…at least when I am around. I was so relieved to hear Linda say that it had been a real joy to have the kids with them.

She raved about Jack telling all kinds of stories with his active imagination. He also worked in the yard with John and helped drive the tractor.

Linda also experienced an "A.J. effect" of her own. I always go to tears when I tell a story about my A.J. and what a sweet boy he is. There is something about his adorable brown eyes and his smile that causes me to well up with tears. Tonight, I was on the receiving end, listening to Linda tell me an A.J. story and hearing her say, "that A.J., what a sweet, sweet boy." Pass the tissue, please.

Of course, she shared a couple of Megan stories, too. I love the way she calls her "Little Kate," or "Megs," or "Miss Megan." As long as Megan gets enough cuddles, she is usually a happy girl. Knowing that Linda has only experienced a limited amount of cuddles from baby girls, I am not surprised to learn that Megan has Linda wrapped around her finger.

Once again from 8,000 miles away, the reports from home are heartwarming. What an encouragement in the midst of the heat, stress, and ongoing difficulties of our trip. The phone calls home have been a lifeline...a cool drink of water in the midst of drought. Prayerfully, we will be able to get home close to on time.

Chapter 9

Part-Time Angels

I do not know how heaven interacts with those of us here on earth. What I do know is that sometimes there are people who show up at just the right time to do just the right thing, and we don't know how we would have survived without their help. Naomi served as our angel in Nairobi, Kenya. We had heard about Naomi from Mandy Sydo, who passed along her name from another family who had adopted a child from Welcome Home. Naomi had helped that family negotiate the immigration process a few months earlier.

Naomi is the daughter of Reverend Solomon M. Mwalili, the pastor of the Free Pentecostal Fellowship in Nairobi. Rev. Mwalili and his family serve the poor by helping young boys get off the Nairobi streets. Their ministry provides food, clothing, and shelter, in addition to teaching the boys some basic skills that will enable them to earn a living.

By Kenyan standards, Naomi had been born into relative wealth and was therefore able to complete university in the United States. She was bright and capable and knew how to work her way through the environment in which she lived. Even before we arrived in Kenya, Naomi was an invaluable resource for us. She made reservations for us at a safe guest house in Nairobi, advised us on how long the girls' physicals would take to process, and was generally a wealth of knowledge. When we realized our arrival in Kenya would be delayed because of the many roadblocks we had experienced, she was able to change our reservations at the guest house.

We arrived in Nairobi around 10:00 p.m., and Naomi and her brother met us at the baggage claim. While clearly tired from a long day at work, they were quick to help us load our heavy bags into their father's old Toyota Land Cruiser. As we started our drive to the guest house, I could easily understand why a tough vehicle like that was needed. On the busy streets of Nairobi, there was a whole new set of rules for the road. There were speed limits, but no police to enforce them. Instead, there were hazardous obstacles placed in the center of the road. If drivers failed to pay attention and negotiate them, the obstacles could easily rip apart tires, damage suspension, or worse. My least favorite obstacle was a "curb" filled with six-inch slanted spikes laying across the middle of the lane that we had to swerve around in an "S." Shortly after the first set of spikes on the right, there was a second set of spikes on the left that we also had to avoid. Needless to say, we did not speed.

The guest house was about forty minutes away from the airport. Naomi and her brother helped us unload our luggage and prepared to head home. Just before they pulled away, Naomi told us she had a few days off from work and would be able to drive us everywhere we needed to go. In reality, at the last minute she had specifically requested several days off so that she could assist us. Little did we know at the time just what a miracle it would be to have Naomi there to help us with the challenges that we would encounter on Tuesday, Wednesday and Thursday. After they left, we hauled our heavy bags up the four flights of stairs to our room. Feeling greatly relieved to finally be together safely in Nairobi, we fell into bed and slept hard. This was the first time we had slept in a cool, dry, comfortable place in more than three weeks. It was the first time Rhoda and Maria had ever slept in such comfortable accommodations. As we slid into the smooth cotton sheets, it occurred to us that most Ugandans, and most Africans for that matter, have never enjoyed such luxuries.

The Physicals

Morning came and we were eager to make our way to the doctor's office to start the process for the physicals. It was recommended that we allow two to three days to process the paperwork and complete the lab work required for the immigration physicals. Originally we had scheduled six days in Kenya. With all the delays, we were hoping to get the physicals processed in twenty-nine hours. Naomi told us not to get our hopes up about getting all of the requirements done that quickly. She said that everything in Kenya, along with most of Africa, followed its own timeline which did not ever move quickly. At the doctor's office, we had heard that if we indicated our timeframe, the doctor and lab would do everything they could to get the paperwork processed and turned around within twenty-four hours, especially for cases involving international travel.

Naomi met us promptly at 9:30 a.m. Feeling fresh and ready for the day, we managed to make our way, twisting and turning through the streets. We arrived at the doctor's office on time, but since we had been delayed several days, they had to work to fit in our appointment. Thankfully, they were willing to squeeze us in first thing.

The nurse called us into the examination room, and the doctor quickly checked both of the girls from head to toe. With the exception of Maria's mild case of scabies, the doctors found the children to be in good overall health. He wrote a prescription for Maria for an ointment to apply every few hours. We also mentioned the chronic diarrhea, and he said they would do a parasite screen on their stool samples. Before leaving the clinic that day, we needed to have urine and stool samples and have their blood drawn. We would also need to return the following day, Wednesday, at 3:30 p.m. to receive the necessary set of vaccinations and meet the courier to collect the final paperwork.

That sounded easy enough. Except that <u>nothing</u> had gone smoothly since we arrived in Africa. I should have expected more of the same. The blood draws were traumatic. Talk about screaming. The girls must have been thinking, *Who are these terrible people? They take me away from my home and hold me down and stick needles in my arm. I don't like this anymore.* Thankfully, they were very forgiving. As soon as we mentioned going to get a treat, they dried their tears and skipped off with us to find some ice cream.

Our next step was to collect the samples. Thankfully, the urine samples were easy, but the stool samples were another matter. We had been trying to slow down the girls' diarrhea by focusing on a BRAT diet (bananas, rice, applesauce, and toast). Rhoda's bowel movements were generally still pretty loose, but Maria's system had actually started to normalize. We knew we had to complete the collection and drop the samples at the doctor's office by 3:00 p.m. in time for the courier to deliver the day's collections to the lab. That gave us two hours. We tried taking the girls to the bathroom several times without success. We tried giving them water. Nothing. We tried fruit smoothies. Nothing. We had them walk up and down the mall stairs, hoping that some exercise might get things moving. Still nothing. An hour-and-a-half went by, and finally we had success with Rhoda. One down, one to go. We only had thirty minutes left or everything would again be delayed. We would not make our flight home, which had already been delayed earlier in the trip. We quickly tried more water, more smoothie, and more walking for Maria. We even tried to tickle her! Finally, I decided to just have her go sit on the toilet. The earlier episode of the push coaching at the Uganda High Court with Maria paid off. She finally went at 2:55 p.m. and the collection was made. Whew! As we turned to leave the doctor's office after making our delivery, the courier walked in. Our specimens were ready for pick up without a minute to spare. Yes!

The next day we returned to the doctor's office to pick up the approvals from the physicals and have a full set of immunization shots administered. More trauma! Mark took Rhoda in first and I could hear the muffled screaming that seemed to last forever. When it was Maria's turn, we went into the room where the needles were visible on a tray. As soon as Maria realized that those needles were going into her body, I literally had to put her in a full body lock to try to keep her still enough for the nurse to inject the vaccinations. Back in Wisconsin, when multiple shots were administered, two nurses would come into the office, each with two needles. The nurses would time the shots: one, two, three go...and then again one, two, three go. It was all over in a matter of seconds. This nurse seemed to take her time, slowly working the needle into the arm or leg, and slowly pushing its contents into the injection site. All the while, Maria was screaming bloody murder. Not only that, Maria and I had to endure this grueling process all over again—three more times! Each needle was literally in the injection site for a full minute. All I could think was: *This is completely unnecessary!*

When we came out of the examination room, we were both exhausted. Rhoda and Mark didn't look much better. What should have been a relatively minor event ended up being one of the most traumatic experiences of the entire trip; we can only imagine what Rhoda and Maria were thinking.

The British Embassy and the Airside Transit Visa

One advantage of managing our own adoption process, rather than working directly with an adoption agency, was that the money we spent on the adoption process covered direct costs, and this kept expenses to a minimum. However, a disadvantage of managing our own adoption was that we didn't know all of the ins and outs of the adoption process. It took us two months to fully realize what we needed to satisfy both the Ugandan and the U.S. governments. In addition, we needed to deal with U.S. Embassies in Uganda and Kenya because all East African immigration was managed at the Embassy in Kenya.

At some point during our time in Uganda, we realized that we might need British Transit Visas for Rhoda and Maria. As U.S. citizens, we did not require transit visas to fly through Heathrow Airport, in London. However, travelers whose passports were issued from an African country needed to have a British Airside Transit Visa in order to land and change planes. Prior to 9/11, it was very easy to complete the paperwork and receive approval to land in Great Britain and then continue on to the final destination. However, the British had tightened up the process for obtaining an Airside Transit Visa, and their new recommendation was to allow four to six days and possibly as long as two weeks to acquire approval. In our case, we needed to make the request on a Tuesday and receive approval by Thursday at the latest.

When we went to the British Embassy, they informed us that we needed to leave the girls' passports with them. That was a problem, because we also needed to have the passports at the U.S. Embassy. How could we simultaneously get exit visas for Rhoda and Maria from the U.S. Embassy and get the process going for the British Airside Transit Visa, both of which required possession of the passports? Further, the work at both embassies could not even be started until the approved paperwork from the physicals arrived, which wouldn't be until be the next day, Wednesday, sometime around 3:30 p.m. Would it be possible to get all of this worked out by Thursday evening so that we could catch our plane?

I decided to call the U.S. Embassy and ask for help with our dilemma. I spoke with Jason Meek, who said they might be able to help us, but he couldn't do anything until we had all the paperwork from the physicals. I also learned that the British Embassy would not process the British Airside Transit Visa until we were granted approval for the exit visas from the U.S. Embassy. Thus, our next step would be to report immediately to the U.S. Embassy when we received the approved paperwork from the physicals.

We returned to the doctor's office the next day to pick up the medical paperwork, which was expected to arrive via courier by about 3:00 p.m. Unfortunately, the courier was late. At 3:50 p.m. the courier still had not yet arrived, and I knew we wouldn't be able to make it to the U.S. Embassy by the 4:00 p.m. closing time. I called and explained the situation to an embassy official, who told us to arrive by 7:00 a.m. on Thursday morning. He also recommended that we call the British Embassy to request an emergency appointment that same morning. By the time the courier arrived, which was just after 4:00 p.m., we had successfully arranged a 10:00 a.m. emergency appointment at the British Embassy. At last, we had the medical paperwork, and we were ready to process our documents at both embassies.

The timing couldn't have been tighter or more stressful. If we were unable to obtain the necessary embassy approvals on Thursday, then document processing and flight scheduling would prevent us from traveling until Monday night, arriving in Chicago at noon on Tuesday, at the earliest. Mark needed to be back to teach his classes, and I couldn't bear the thought of further delays—I needed to get home to see Megan and her brothers! We said a prayer, "God, we really need your help."

On Thursday, Naomi arrived at the Mercy guest house at 6:45 a.m. The embassy was supposed to be a quick fifteen-minute drive away, but as we headed out, we realized that the early morning traffic was much heavier than we had expected. To make matters worse, we noticed steam coming out the front end of Naomi's navy blue Volkswagen. Her car was overheating. Naomi pulled her troubled car out of the bustling traffic into a church parking lot. Mark called the taxi driver that we had used a couple of times, and he picked us up fifteen minutes later. We managed to get to the U.S. Embassy by 8:00 a.m. We worked our way through the lengthy security line and walked into the embassy waiting area. It was packed! How would we ever obtain the necessary approvals AND get over to our 10:00 a.m. appointment at the British Embassy, which was thirty minutes away?

As I considered all the cumulative levels of stress we experienced during this trip, I thought, *This is taking about five years off of my life.*

We took a number, found a seat, and waited. There was nothing else we could do. The power was not in our hands. We could only submit to the procedures, requirements, and laws. Those in authority would ultimately determine whether we would be leaving on our flight later that evening. It was 9:20 a.m. before we were called to the counter. I had all of the paperwork in order so that they could quickly handle our request. The clerk completed our documents efficiently, but before she took the passports, I asked to speak with Jason Meek. Jason was the embassy official I had spoken with by phone on Tuesday. He was a tall, lean man with a friendly demeanor, and his Midwest accent gave him away. As he looked over our paperwork, he noticed our Wisconsin address and said that he was from Stevens Point, Wisconsin. That probably didn't make a difference, but I felt a surge of hope that he would do everything in his power to clear a path for us. He took our paperwork but let us keep the passports, which were needed at the British Embassy. He then gave us a letter indicating that our exit visas would be approved later in the day. Then he told us to call him if we had any trouble acquiring the Airside Transit Visa. Thank you, Jason!

It was 9:45 a.m. and Naomi had fixed her car and was ready to run us over to the British Embassy. We arrived ten minutes late for our appointment and, though curt, they did allow the four of us into the embassy. Thankfully, this time there were only few people in the waiting area. I went up to the service window and turned in the paperwork that we had completed earlier in the week, along with Jason's letter, the crisp new U.S. currency, the passports, and the appropriately sized photos. Remember the first batch of visa photos we picked up back in Jinja? It turned out that the smaller sized photos were exactly what we would need for the British Airside Transit Visa, while the second larger photos were required for the U.S. Embassy exit visas. We were thankful for that earlier "error," which in reality was a miraculous blessing.

The clerk took everything from me without a word. At the risk of appearing overtly assertive, I explained our need to get the visa that day, with enough time to get back to the U.S. Embassy for passport stamping, so that we could travel on our 11:20 p.m. flight later that evening. She just looked at me and told me to have a seat in the waiting area.

We waited. By 11:00 a.m. the other two groups of people that had been in the waiting area when we arrived had completed their business and left. In my mind, that meant that we were next and our situation would hopefully be resolved soon. Another hour went by. It was getting to be lunchtime and the girls were hungry and restless, so Mark left with Rhoda and Maria to meet Naomi and find some lunch. Once Mark exited the embassy, he would not be permitted to return. It seemed that it shouldn't take too much longer and we would be on our way, so I was fine waiting the remainder of the time on my own.

At about 12:30 p.m., Mr. Edna Mwandoe came out to talk with me. He was a tall, imposing figure. He was quite stern and clearly expressed, in his strong British accent, that he didn't appreciate our emergency request for an Airside Transit Visa. I agreed with him that from his perspective it might not seem appropriate for us to make such a request. I explained that we originally were scheduled to have a full six days in Nairobi, which would have given us sufficient time to follow the standard procedures. Since he appeared to be willing to hear me out, I went on to explain the delayed court date, the delayed court order, the last minute orphan investigation, and then the missing court ruling, all of which required us to stay in Uganda a week longer than expected. I told him that if it were just Mark, me, and the girls, we would be willing to go through the regular process. But we had six-year-old Jack, three-year-old A.J., and one-year-old Megan back in the United States with Grandma. I told him that we had already been gone since January 4, and we just couldn't bear yet another delay, especially for an Airside Transit Visa: At Heathrow, we simply needed to walk off our plane from Nairobi and on to the next plane for our flight to Chicago, Illinois. We didn't even have a layover.

I'm sure the guy must have been thinking: *take a breath, lady!* His face did soften a bit, and as he left the room he said, "I will see what I can do." This time he sounded more like he was trying to sound stern. Before the door closed, I also quickly reminded him of the letter from the U.S. Embassy and mentioned that he could call Jason Meek to confirm that they were going to be stamping the girls' passport visas as soon we returned, this afternoon. I went back to waiting, feeling a little more hopeful and relieved since I was able plea our case.

Finally, at 1:50 p.m., Officer Mwandoe let me know that he had spoken with Mr. Meek and everything looked OK. I breathed a sigh of relief, but I was still mindful that I needed to actually get the paperwork in hand with enough time to make it back to the U.S. Embassy, hopefully by 3:00 p.m. I tried to distract myself, but I was pacing and my heart was racing. At last, the security door opened again. It was Mr. Mwandoe. I stood up and looked him squarely in the eye with a hopeful expectation. He then handed me the approved paperwork and stamped passports. Huge tears began rolling down my cheeks as I accepted the precious papers. Attempting to regain my composure, I said, "Thank you. Thank you so very much." Then I asked him if I could give him a hug. He nodded his head, yes, so I gave him a great big hug, saying thank you one more time. This time, when I looked up at his handsome brown face, there were tears in his eyes. He gently said, "I know. I know." I nodded my head, gave him a warm appreciative smile and ran out the door to meet Mark, Naomi, and the girls.

At 2:47 p.m. we were off to jump through the last pre-travel hoop. The city traffic was getting congested again, but Naomi drove as fast as the traffic, roads, and obstacles permitted. We made it to within sight of the embassy, when the traffic came to a standstill. Mark jumped out of the car saying, "I am just going to run there." With the paperwork in his backpack, he ran the last half mile despite the ninety degree temperature. He arrived at the embassy, passed once again through security, took a number, and sat down to wait for the next available clerk. Thankfully, the queue was short and Mark was called to the counter with time to spare. He was sure to thank Jason Meek for all his help (but he did not give him a hug). The exit visas were granted and passports stamped. We did it! We officially had everything we needed to travel on our 11:20 p.m. flight that evening.

Chapter 10

Traveling Home

After an enjoyable evening with Naomi's family, we made our way to the airport. We had all the necessary documents, and we felt very relaxed, overall. As we waited to check in at the international ticket counter, I pulled out and reviewed all of the documents: the tickets, passports, visas, birth certificates, etc. Then I stopped short. I couldn't believe what I saw! Rhoda's name on her passport was different than her name on the plane ticket and birth certificate. The passport read, "Rhoda Kemigisha Hodgkin." On the plane ticket and birth certificate, it was "Rhoda Hodgkin Kemigisha." Would the officials allow us through?

When we came up to the ticketing agent, we decided not to say anything. He took our tickets, passports, and support documents. He spent a few minutes looking, clicking, and stamping. Then without making eye contact he pointed to the customer service window and told us to go there. We moved our two luggage carts with the girls riding on top and waited in yet another line. At the counter, the agent reached over and took all of our documents. I nervously broke into a long explanation about how the ticket name and the birth certificate name were the correct but that the passport had the middle and last named reversed. He looked blankly at me and asked if I had said something. I decided to say no. Again he looked, clicked, stamped, pointed, and sent us on our way to the security entrance. I quickly scooped up the documents with yet another sigh of relief, and we headed for the security checkpoint.

We had to go to a special counter because we were bringing the girls out of the country. The woman took our documents and asked, "Where are the original birth certificates?" I was puzzled, because I thought we had the original birth certificates. She informed me that they were only certified copies. With panic in my voice, I explained that we had used them with the High Court in Uganda, the British Embassy, and the U.S. Embassies in both Uganda and Kenya. She stared at the full set of documents for what seemed like forever. Without looking at us or saying another word, she stamped the necessary approvals and passed everything back to us. Finally, we were through security and on our way home.

As we sat down at our gate to wait for our flight, we finally had a chance to look at our seat assignments. Knowing that we had delayed our original departure by two days, we doubted we would be able to sit all four together, but we were surprised to find that our seat assignments were nowhere near each other. We inquired at the ticket counter to see if we could get reassigned and they said, "No. You will just have to wait until you board the plane. Talk to a stewardess to see if it will be possible to at least arrange seats so that each child could be with one adult."

The girls were new to flying and it seemed likely that they would break into a bout of crying and screaming if they were left to fend for themselves. In the interest of every passenger on the plane, it seemed like a reasonable request to have us sit two and two. The stewardess set us aside and asked us to wait while she made arrangements for a switch. After fifteen minutes, she returned to tell us that none of the 300+ passengers on the plane were willing to switch seats. Unbelievable. Mark said, "That's ok. Let's start with our separate seats. I am sure that once the screaming begins, a few passengers will have a change of heart."

Apparently, that was enough to motivate a few passengers to change seats, because the stewardess returned a few minutes later with new seat assignments. I sat with Maria in one part of the plane, and Mark sat with Rhoda in another part of the plane. Surprisingly, the girls were very settled. They didn't scream and actually slept most of the long flight to Heathrow. The transfer of planes at Heathrow went smoothly too. Thankfully, we had the British Airside Transit Visas as they were in fact needed to get the girls off the plane in London. We made our way to our next plane and soon we were off to Chicago. Fortunately, our seats were all together on the second flight.

As we got closer to home, our thoughts turned to the decisions we had set aside when we left. The job invitation from Michigan State University still required an answer, and the application deadline was the Monday after we returned home. It was a unique opportunity, one that might not come along over the course of an entire career. We figured that applying for a job was very different from actually taking a new job, and we could always withdraw the application if we changed our minds. Thus, we decided that Mark would throw his hat in the ring.

Home!

We shared a huge sigh of relief when we touched down in Chicago. It felt so good to be home! Our last hurdle was getting through immigration and customs. The line was long, and it took what felt like an eternity to get through. When it was finally our turn, we showed the officials our passports and passed them the immigration envelope. Two security guards were called over to our booth, and they asked us to follow them. My first thought was that we were being detained. Yet as we followed the guards, they didn't seem to be taking us anywhere in particular. Finally, they stopped at a booth on the far side of the customs area. One of the officers leaned over the wall of the booth to reach for a special sticker to put on the outside of our immigration envelope. After placing the sticker carefully on the envelope, he looked up and said, "Thank you. You're all set. Welcome to the United States, girls." I'm sure I had a look of complete surprise on my face. We quickly moved forward to the baggage claim area before anybody could change their mind.

Our suitcases were already circling around on the baggage carousel, so we piled them high onto a cart. With emotions beginning to surge, I carried Maria and headed toward the exit. With Rhoda riding on top, Mark pushed the cart through the big heavy steel doors that brought us onto official U.S. soil. I was so happy to be back in the United States! I felt as if I could kiss the ground.

With more urgent priorities, I scanned the area for the faces of Jack, A.J., and Megan, but didn't see them anywhere. I then realized that there were two sets of exit doors, and the members of our welcoming party were all standing at the other exit. We walked up from behind, completely surprising everyone. My eyes zoomed in on Megan wearing a cute blue romper and sporting adorable, puffy piggy tails. She looked so grown up. At her age, a month was a very long time to be away. Tears started to flow. Still holding Maria, I sat down to hug Megan while Mark, holding Rhoda, gave Jack and A.J. a great big bear hug. In moments, my lap was filled with the very shy Maria, Megan, and Jack and A.J. wiggling their way on too. My sister, Elizabeth, snapped pictures while my nephews Christian and Joshua welcomed Rhoda and Maria, passing them each an adorable doll. My mom, surprised that we had come from behind, looked both happy and relieved that we had made it home. My friend Carrie stood there amazed, hardly knowing what to think of the whole scene. I was overcome with emotion as the reality of finally being home together with everyone sunk in. To get us right back into the swing of things, Megan beckoned for a diaper change. Mark volunteered to take her, while I smothered hugs and kisses on Jack and A.J. with Rhoda and Maria snuggled all around me. Thank you God! We made it. We were home.

The weather in Chicago at 2:30 p.m. on January 27, 2006, was sunny, windy, and cold. The temperature was in the twenties, but the wind made it feel much colder. The seventy degree temperature change was a shock for all of us but even more so for Rhoda and Maria who had no concept of their body freezing when exposed to the cold. There were winter coats in the van for them to wear, but they did not want to put them on. Instead we cranked up the heat. Mark and I, along with our five kids, drove the 100 miles back home in our van. Mom, Christian, and Joshua rode with Elizabeth in her van. It was difficult to say goodbye to Carrie so soon, but she lived just a short distance from O'Hare and wouldn't be making the trip to Wisconsin, where the welcome home party was to continue.

During the drive, all of the kids were chattering back and forth. We also had some music CD's that both sets of kids were familiar with, so they also sang together. I was elated to be home, and I was deeply joyful about our expanded brood. The twenty-three days in Africa gave Mark and me a lot of focused time that enabled us to bond with Rhoda and Maria. We were thankful for that period together. Yet, twenty-three days was also a very long time to be away from Jack, A.J., and Megan. I couldn't wait to reconnect with them.

After we arrived at our home in Whitewater, though travel weary, we were all buzzing with excitement. Elizabeth offered to give Rhoda and Maria a bubble bath to clean them up from the travel grime. The girls were happy to soak and play in the tub. It was their first real bubble bath in warm sudsy water, and they smiled bigger and laughed harder than we had seen to date. Remember Maria, the girl who didn't smile? After the bath, my sister said, "Maria's smile is so big she looks as if she just won the lottery!" Like a flower blooming for the first time, her smile opened up and was brighter than I had ever seen. Almost four years later, her smile still shines brightly.

Redefining Normal

As expected, the first few hours, days, weeks, and months of our new and improved family design were filled with interesting transitions. Helping everyone regain their footing was both hard and rewarding. The first bedtime was interesting. We put Rhoda and Maria in their new room, in their new beds, kissed them good night, and partly closed the door. It was one of many situations where screaming ensued. We tried again. In an attempt to help them transition, we put all five kids in one room. Rhoda and Maria were familiar with sleeping with many children in a room, so perhaps being in the room by themselves felt more like a punishment. After two weeks of all the kids sharing a room, screaming or no screaming, we decided it was time to move everyone into their planned sleep space. Eventually we "won," and everyone was able to finally go to sleep in their own bed.

A second major transition was with our dog, Niko. Our wonderful friend and neighbor, Donna, watched Niko the entire time we were in Africa and kept her an additional month after we returned. Hoping to transition Niko back into our home sooner rather than later, Donna would bring her to the house for visits. The first few visits were awful. Rhoda and Maria were terrified of dogs and screamed their heads off at the sight of Niko. Rhoda looked seriously terrified and would scramble backwards as quickly as possible to get away from her. After almost four weeks of trying to get the girls accustomed to the idea that Niko was their dog too and that she would be coming home to stay with us soon, we had made very little progress with their adjustment. Mark decided that we needed to try full emersion. I was feeling pessimistic, but I agreed that we needed to give it our best shot because Niko was our pup and we loved her and wanted to keep her in our family. Besides, in the United States, dogs were everywhere. The girls either had to get used to them or live in fear just about everywhere we went. The first two days were literally a scream fest, especially for Rhoda. If Niko was in the room, even if she was just laying there sleeping peacefully, both girls would scream and scream. After a few weeks, Maria finally warmed up to Niko and began playing catch with her. Rhoda continued to scream several weeks longer, but even she slowly acclimated to Niko and eventually came to love her too. One day she asked if she could adopt Niko as her own pet. She wanted the responsibility of feeding, watering, and walking her. We were very thankful to finally achieve this successful transition.

As we settled into home and routine, my new motto became, "There is always room [on my lap] for one more." I didn't want anyone to feel like they needed to compete for "mom time." If I had three kids on my lap already, I was quick to include numbers four and five if they wanted "up" too. I sat less in my recliner, which quickly ran out of space, favoring the couch where there was room for everyone to be touching me at once.

About six months after we arrived home, we were all finally beginning to feel fairly well adjusted. Rhoda and Maria were making progress with speaking English. The improved communications meant that the frustration levels were coming down. The bedtime screaming was less frequent. Sanity was slowly returning, and Mark and I were actually beginning to sleep again at night. One day in late August, not long after Mark and I returned from our tenth anniversary get away, I walked up three flights of stairs at work feeling terribly out of breath. I thought to myself, *in the past when I felt this out of breath walking up these stairs, I was pregnant.* But that wasn't possible, was it?

After several days of feeling funky, I told Mark, "I've been feeling odd, almost like I'm pregnant."

Mark looked at me with alarm and said, "Do you think?"

I decided to confirm that I was indeed not pregnant with a home pregnancy test. The first test came up positive, so I quickly opened the second test and tried again. Staring at the positive results on both tests, I realized, "Wow! We are really going to have a baby!" Mark and I looked at each other and laughed. Jack was going to get his wish after all—he was going to have five brothers and sisters.

Luke Anthony was born on April 27, 2007. He was a healthy, beautiful, fair-haired boy. We had achieved balance in our family: Three boys and three girls; three with brown eyes and three with blue eyes; three brown-haired kids and three sandy-haired kids. Luke also served to create a common bond among the children. The even numbers meant that everyone had a partner: when the kids paired off to play, it was Jack and A.J., Maria and Megan, Rhoda and Luke. They all had an engaging little brother to share, to care for, to play with, to laugh with, and to hug. Rhoda, Maria, and Megan experienced for the first time how families grow, the old fashioned way. Luke rounded us off to an even number. I will certainly never forget our amazing tenth wedding anniversary gift to one another. God, in his wisdom, had sent us this unexpected and blessed gift.

Chapter 11

The Children Today

Now two years of age, Luke is a capable little guy, and funny too. At his leading, he was potty trained when he was twenty-two months old. He has a great sense of humor, always providing some comic relief. Recently, Mark had taken him into our bathroom to brush his teeth. On the way out, he asked Luke to go to our closet to get a diaper for bedtime. As he went into the closet, Mark turned off the bathroom light and began to walk over to turn on a light by the bed. For a moment, it was very dark. Just then, seven-year-old A.J. walked into the room to drop his dirty clothes into the laundry basket. As he came through our door, Luke jumped out of the closet with a loud ROAR! Mark turned on the light to see a startled A.J. and a smiling Luke. A.J. laughed and said, "Whoa, Lukey really did scare me!" Mark said, "He scared me too!" Even at two years of age, Luke likes to tease and joke. He helps us to not take life and the challenges quite so seriously.

Jack and A.J. are great big brothers. Jack, now nine, is a doer. He likes to keep busy and is a great help. While we try not to rely on him too much, he is always there to help. He has a great imagination and is always finding a new adventure. He is also a natural protector. Not long after Rhoda and Maria had arrived home, the kids were all playing in the basement. Jack, just barely six at the time, walked up stairs with a set of Exacto knives that Rhoda had somehow pulled out of a box. She was playing with them! Jack took the knives, walked up the stairs, and gave them to me. He said, "Rhoda was playing with these. I thought I'd better give them to you." Jack intervened on more than one occasion.

While Jack is action oriented, A.J. is more introspective. One time when he was two years old, I dressed him up in his snowsuit to go out and play in the falling snow. A.J. went out on the back deck, sat down, and watched the snow for fifteen minutes. When he finally came in, I asked him, "What were you doing out there, A.J.?" He replied, "Just watching the snow fall." This impressed me so much because in Jack's four years I had not ever seen him sit down to watch anything for fifteen minutes. He would have been rolling, jumping, and playing in the snow. A.J. is also a very patient teacher. Oftentimes, Rhoda will resist when Mark or I try to have her read to us. When that happens, we call in A.J. With his easygoing personality, he just seems to connect with Rhoda so that she will read to him.

When we first arrived home with the girls, Megan had a harder time with the transition. She missed us when we were away for so long in Africa, and she wasn't old enough to completely understand what was happening. All she knew was that when we returned, she had to share her momma with two other girls. No fair! Early on, she would wake up in the morning and see Rhoda and Maria and look at them with an expression that said, "Do you mean to tell me that you girls are still here?" In time, she made the transition and now loves her sisters. From the beginning, they all wanted to sleep in same room together, which has caused us some trouble. Any one girl, by herself, is pretty low key and manageable. Each girl seems to manage her responsibilities pretty well as long as she isn't distracted by the others. Get any two of them together, however, and you start to feel the energy level rise. Three of them together results in some sort of chemical reaction: The noise increases, and the girls' ability to follow directions of any kind diminishes. My survival motto when it comes to completing chores, getting ready for bed, etc., is "divide and conquer."

Since coming home with us, Maria has undergone a major personality shift. At this point, I would not use the word "quiet" to describe her. She is a very happy girl and definitely very capable. She loves to sing and has a natural inclination toward music. In fact, she seems to have a special talent in this area. When she was four years old, she started taking violin lessons. One evening shortly after we began the lessons, our family watched the movie *Rocky III*. After the movie, she pulled out her violin, plucked on it for a few minutes, and then played the theme song, *Eye of the Tiger*. Amazing. Maria also appreciates all things of beauty and sees the world with an artist's perspective. She is quick to prefer the beautiful flowered sheets to the plain old solid color ones, and she is willing to endure the time and the pain involved in braiding her hair because she loves how it looks. Whenever she visits Aunt Elizabeth, she requests to have her fingernails and toenails painted. A friend of mine once said, "I love Maria. She lives her life in **boldface**."

The following paragraphs about Maria were written by Erika Briedis, a friend and babysitter in the United States

"Rhoda, Rhoda," cries Maria to her playmate as she skips down the hall. During the summer, my sisters and I take turns watching Rhoda and Maria, a pair of Ugandan girls who were adopted by our friends.

Maria, with wide, wondering brown eyes and a smiling mouth, is a sweet girl. She loves to sing and dance. At the slightest encouragement she happily twirls and jumps around the room mumbling to herself, singing snatches of a familiar song.

At the orphanage they only wore dresses on very special occasions. So Maria also loves to dress up, and dancing in a "pretty" dress is one of her favorite things to do.

Every girl at the orphanage had a sort of "buzz cut" so that it was easier to take care of the girls' hair. When Maria first came to the United States, her brown eyes grew wide with amazement as she looked at the brown and blonde long hair of my sisters and me. She was sad that her own hair couldn't be so long and pretty, so we tied a sheet or sometimes a towel around her head, which she would stroke and say, "look, look at my pretty hair." Since then her hair has grown, and she was ecstatic when our friends took her to the hair salon for the first time.

Another one of her chief loves is her "poppa." She jabbers about him and asks repeatedly when he'll be home. When any stranger walks into the room, Maria dashes for her father's legs for refuge; peeking out, she watches the new visitor. After awhile you can soon find her in the stranger's arms.

She also loves to swing and begs us to push her for the twenty millionth time.

She loves to show people her things. "Look, look!" she always cries to draw my attention back to her, when I'm distracted by something else.

Outside of her blue house in a little kettle surrounded by pine trees, Maria hunches down and draws several lines of yellow chalk on the pavement. She straightens up and shuffles from one foot to the other, then twirls and falls back to her chalk scribbling. Finishing, she stands up and puts her hands behind her back and, looking up at me, points at her drawing.

"Erika, Erika look, look at my drawing."

"Good job Maria! What is it?"

"It's a yellow flower."

She puts her arms out to me and I pick her up, her piece of chalk still in her hand. She's only four but she keeps getting heavier every year. She scoots up and puts her arms around my neck and squeezes; I can feel the chalk rubbing against by neck. She leans her head against my shoulder and her "pretty" pigtail buds brush my cheek—her hair feels almost like a berber rug. I put her down as she starts squirming when she sees Rhoda scrambling for the scooter. I love to watch her play. Maria Mikayla is one of the sweetest little girls there is.

As Maria blossomed, Rhoda seemed to settle down. At the orphanage, Rhoda had developed two strategies for getting the attention she craved. The first approach was to turn on her charm and shine like the sun. She would often run over and give that radiant smile and then lean in to be picked up and carried. She loved to be carried! However, if for some reason things didn't go her way, she would often provide a fantastic show: The temper tantrums and screaming were frequently enough to cause the mums at Welcome Home to acquiesce. As she settled into life in our family, she realized that she didn't have to turn on the charm to get the attention she needed. Her bright smiles became less show and more authentic. She went from hugging anyone and everyone to telling people that she does not know them well enough for them to touch her. On the other hand, even though we are pretty firm with her, she still attempts to use the tantrum and screaming strategy. After a major tantrum, I often step into the bedroom where she has been sent and ask her, "Rhoda, in our home, has screaming ever gotten you what you wanted?" Rhoda typically responds with a quiet, "No." To which I say, "Then why continue to scream? It only means that you get sent to your room and lose privileges." Rhoda will say, "I know." Major transitions are still a challenge for her, but advanced warning is a big help. Slowly, she is learning more healthy behavioral patterns.

Rhoda has made progress with her health issues as well. Over the last several years she has gone through physical therapy, speech therapy, and occupational therapy as well as surgery to lengthen the heel chord on her left leg. She is a very brave, determined, and tough girl. Her physical therapist often notes how hard she works. Now, at seven years old, she can run a mile, ride a bike, and speak clearly. The brain is incredible: Given the proper stimuli, it can develop new neural pathways that bypass many damaged areas. Though Rhoda will likely require various forms of medical monitoring through the years, we are thankful to report that she is functioning so much more effectively. When we see Rhoda's sunshine smile, it reminds us how much we have all been blessed by her addition to our family. We are glad for the opportunity to help her become all that God has planned in her special life.

What about MSU?

After we returned home from Africa, Mark applied for the job at Michigan State University. A few weeks after he submitted his application, I changed my mind. I didn't want to leave Whitewater, WI. The timing didn't seem right to me. Going from three to five children was stressful, and I wanted to stay in the familiar environment that I loved, where our support system was established.

When I learned I was pregnant with Luke, I was even more convinced that this was not the time to move.

Even though the costs of moving were high, Mark wanted to play it out. "Let's just see what happens," he said. He believed that maybe the move would be good for the family in the long run. It was a long ten months between the time Mark applied for the position and when he received the job offer. We would be moving to Michigan.

Through the intense times, I thank God every day that he sent Luke when he did. With a baby in tow, I had to focus on staying closely connected to my tender, gentle, nurturing side. We moved to Michigan on Father's Day, June 17, 2007, when Luke was just two months old. Going from three to six children, with a major move, in just 18 months pushed the limits of the load I felt I could bear. Through it all, the children calmed me; their smiles healed me; their snuggles settled me; their laughs lifted me. Luke served as a reprieve from the busy household activity when I nursed him upstairs alone in my bedroom. As I sat cuddling him in my chair, I drank in the beautiful fall colors outside my new window. This retreat washed my mind and helped me stay focused on the beauty of this period; this happy, intense, fun, overwhelming, blessed time in my life. I couldn't help but draw strength from the chorus of the song "Evidence of Love" that was sung at our wedding (First Call 1993).

> *Open your eyes and look upon the handiwork of God*
> *Open your soul and feel the breath of glory all around*
> *For everywhere there's evidence of love*

In Closing

We encountered many challenges along our path, but we are honored and very blessed by our children. Through it all, God has faithfully met our needs. We hope that this account encourages others to consider the plight of the world's orphans. According to a report by UNICEF, there are more than 163 million orphans worldwide (UNICEF 2009). Most orphans live in the developing world where their parents have died due to violence, famine, or disease. While

Asia has the greatest number of orphans at 82 million, Africa has the highest percentage of orphans—about twelve percent of all children are orphaned. That number is astounding: 163 million orphans in the world. Wow. What can one family do to help? It seems overwhelming. But think of it this way. About seventy-three percent of the world's 6.8 billion people are adults. If one in every thirty adults (or about one in fifteen couples) cared for a child, every orphan would have a family, and much suffering could be alleviated. Of course, we know that for a number of reasons not all adults are in a position to support a child. However, for families who are interested in adoption but are without the financial resources needed, organizations such as Show Hope offer adoption grants. Whenever possible, orphans should be placed within their own extended families. In Uganda, untold numbers of grandparents, aunts and uncles, friends, and other family members adopt and care for orphans. Unfortunately, extended families all too often do not have the means to take in and care for additional children.

Organizations such as Welcome Home and Nyaka Aids Orphan School do much to help families and villages care for children in need, giving children hope. Welcome Home not only cares for orphans, it engages in many activities designed to build self-sustaining social systems: health care, education, micro-loans, and the creation of business/income generating opportunities. As described by our friend Jackson Kaguri in his book *The Price of Stones*, Nyaka Aids Orphan School is an excellent example of a courageous effort to build one village's capacity to care for and educate orphaned children (Kaguri and Linville 2009). We are overwhelmed by the courage of those who step in to care for children or help build the capacity of communities to care for children, often in the most difficult of circumstances. It's difficult to argue with James:

> "Religion that God our Father accepts as pure and
> faultless is this: to look after orphans and widows
> in their distress..." -James 1:27$_{NIV}$

If a person ever wanted to make a difference in the world, caring for orphans or assisting those who care for orphans seems like a pretty sure bet. Each of us can do something: Pray; sponsor a child; serve at or financially support an orphanage; help remove financial barriers for families seeking adoption; find ways to assist families and even cultures in overcoming the destructive patterns that result in poverty and violence. There are many organizations that do much to build self-sufficiency and eradicate poverty and violence. Look for organizations that build capacity, not dependency, in the countries where they work. Contact information for the organizations we encountered and/or support is provided in the appendix. After all, what does it hurt to just ask a few questions?

An Invitation

Have you received an invitation in your life? If so, would you like to share your story? Perhaps you're not yet sure about your invitation. Would you like to begin a conversation? Maybe you have heard your invitation, but feel stuck and don't know how to actually move forward. If you would like to participate in The Invitation Community, please contact us at theinvitationstory@gmail.com. We will do our best to encourage, inspire, and connect you with possible resources to help you move forward in *your* invitation story.

It is our hope that as the Invitation Community shares its stories, a greater number of people will tune in to their invitations and begin their own journeys.

Imagine what the collective impact might be if we all responded.

Laus Deo

Afterword

We have kept in contact with Mandy Sydo since our trip to Welcome Home in January 2006. She has kept us abreast of the continued improvements to the orphanage, stories of families adopting other children, updates on employees, and the comprehensive development strategies they employ to serve the children, the families, the staff, and the villages throughout Uganda. Below are excerpts from a recent letter from Mandy.

I wish you and Mark could see the tremendous changes that have happened in the home since you were there in January 2006. I know you would love watching the long-term change in the lives that have happened all the way along as the home and the people have grown.

The home still needs more improvements but it is very different from when you were there. Joseph is doing a great job as manager. The ministry has been sending Joseph to school for the past two years. This year he will be graduating from high school and there is a possibility that he may go on to college. He has just started to train an assistant, which is not an easy adjustment for him. His response was to fear for his job. I have asked him to trust me. Schooling is so important to help solidify change.

Our nurse, who used to do our laundry, and our new social worker we have put through their schooling too. They are very proud of their graduation and are becoming good leaders. The social worker works with the legalities of the children's admission, return home transfer or adoptions. She also works with the outreach team and keeps an eye out for village children in need of medical services or rescue. Rhoda started a lot of ministry to hydrocephalic children and their mothers. We give them some hope and make the travel for surgery possible. Our practical nurse watches over the health of the kids and interfaces with the medical clinics and hospitals. We are so thankful for the decrease in the number of deaths. Good clinics have helped, but most of it is because of better care in the home and more hand washing.

In addition to Joseph's assistant, the practical nurse and the social worker, we have also added a new pastor. The pastor once worked for us as the gate keeper for the home. He left for two years to street preach and has now returned to serve the home and head up the outreach to the villages. We have four motorcycles with eight staff serving the village, hospital and prison ministries five days a week.

I think the biggest difference at the home is that now the Ugandans have pride of ownership. It is fully Ugandan run. It is their home and they are demanding high standards of each other. The workers are much stronger in their faith in Christ and believe the Lord for miracles in the children all the time. I have the home on an adequate budget so now there is no shortage of toilet paper. In fact, there are plenty of rolls of TP for the mums to wipe noses along with liquid soap at all the sinks ninety-five percent of the time. We are working on the other five percent of the time.

The head mum is now Grace. She is very demanding of good work to be done and has everyone working hard. She is tough but kind and the kids respect her and love her. Unfortunately, there has been turnover in some of the staff who were unwilling to give up their lazy ways. One of the vacancies brought us Christine to fill the role of head toddler mum and teacher. She has been a real blessing to the home. Rachel has now been promoted to head mum of the bigger babies and is doing an excellent job. The mums work really hard with the kids to stimulate them in their early development. They read to them, play puzzles, do physiotherapy, and teach them to talk. It is special to see how much of the staff love and cuddle all of the children.

I give suggestions to the head mums of where they need to pull their team up and give a nice bonus when they get a breakthrough. It is working well, and they police themselves and help each other. Of course they love the bonus. I have ways of showing appreciation to the rest of the staff as well. The other staff are rewarded according to the reports I get and also to the effort I see them put in. All of their pay is done by direct deposit into bank accounts that we opened for all of them. They are learning to save and pay their own way. If they save half the funds to buy a bike, we pay the other half. Each year it is very easy to see the improvements.

The big babies now have their own special fenced in playground on the right side of the driveway under the trees. It is great for the kids and the mums. This leaves the largest part of the yard with the swings, slide, and trampoline for the bigger kids. We also built a sunroom off the front of the preemie house that Mumma Joy loves. It is screened in so there are no flies on the babies. Joy says it is the best thing we have ever done for her kids. Also our new preschool room is also nearly completed. This new classroom will make teaching the children's classes much easier.

Many of the staff and families of our children have been granted small business micro loans through my home church. These loans have transformed the lives of many families. Because of the availability of these loans, many of our staff now own side businesses. They have been able to build their own home back in the village and now have the funds to help their families. The women always pay back their loans. Unfortunately, I cannot say the same for the men.

June 2010 brings a new aspect of village ministry as two of our Ugandan board members, both graduates of Fuller Seminary in California, come back to work alongside Welcome Home with ministry to village pastors and leaders who are unable to afford an education. They support their own ministry, but it is an investment in our ministry. It is wonderful to have the privilege to minister and to make a difference for the children, but also for the villages from which they came.

Having been in Uganda and at the orphanage for almost three weeks, I can tell you that even maintaining the daily operations of the orphanage is a major accomplishment. The comprehensive list of initiatives achieved—including the investment in the development and education of the staff, the remodeling and expansion of facilities, and the growth of the outreach to the village ministry, along with meeting the needs of daily operations—is astounding. Welcome Home is bringing about real change in lives and in communities all around Jinja. It is an excellent example of an integrative approach to serving and building capacity in the developing world.

References

Dr. Seuss' Horton Hears a Who. Directed by Jimmy Hayward and Steve Martino. 2008; Los Angeles, CA: 20th Century Fox.

First Call. "Evidence of Love." *Sacred Journey.* Birdwing Music (a div. of the Sparrow Corp.). 1993. CD.

Kaguri, Jackson Twesigye and Susan Urbanek Linville. 2009. *The Price of Stones: Building a School for My Village.* New York: Viking Press.

United Nations Children' Fund (UNICEF). 2009. *The State of the World's Children: Special Report.* New York: United Nations.

Organizations Serving Orphans

(Related to our story)

CURE Children's Hospital of Uganda
PO Box 903, Mbale, Uganda (Mailing Address)
Plot 97-105, Bugwere Road, Mbale, Uganda (physical address)
Tel: 256-45-44-35273
Fax: 256-45-44-35355
info@cureuganda.org

CURE Children's Hospital of Uganda is a specialized children's neurosurgery hospital in Uganda. It is a private hospital, owned and operated by CURE International. The hospital is also a teaching center in pediatric neurosurgery for Sub-Saharan Africa.

Embakasi Church–Uzima Centre
http://streetchildren.kardsafrica.org/

Nyaka Aids Orphan School
http://www.nyakaschool.org/
Working to free orphans from the cycle of poverty.

Samaritans Purse
http://www.samaritanspurse.org/
Samaritan's Purse is a nondenominational evangelical Christian organization providing spiritual and physical aid to hurting people around the world. Since 1970, Samaritan's Purse has helped meet needs of people who are victims of war, poverty, natural disasters, disease, and famine with the purpose of sharing God's love through His Son, Jesus Christ.

Show Hope: A Movement to Care for Orphans

http://www.showhope.org/

Show Hope is dedicated to engaging the church to care for orphans and reducing the financial barriers to adoption. This means that we are actively involved in three areas:

1. Adoption Aid: providing waiting orphans with loving families by financially assisting adoptive couples through adoption grants.

2. Orphan Care: participating in orphan care projects that address the holistic needs of orphans—physically, emotionally and spiritually, with the ultimate goal of helping to place the child in the best permanent situation possible, ideally a forever family.

3. Getting Involved: mobilizing individuals and communities to care for orphans through our Adoption Aid and Orphan Care programs.

Welcome Home Africa Orphanage

http://www.welcomehomeafrica.org/

1. To care for the children of Uganda who are orphans, sick, dying, abused, abandoned, or neglected who have no chance of survival without intervention.

2. Provide a loving life-giving environment to give each child a healthy secure foundation for life teaching them about God's love for them.

World Vision

http://www.worldvision.org/

World Vision is a Christian humanitarian organization dedicated to working with children, families, and their communities worldwide to reach their full potential by tackling the causes of poverty and injustice.

Resources Mentioned

Topplers   www.topplers.org

Setting big things in motion one person at a time.

LaVergne, TN USA
22 January 2011
213508LV00001B/5/P